Dying and Grieving

HOW TO COMFORT THOSE IN PAIN

By Dr. Frederic B. Tate

MAGNI

Website: www.magnico.com

ISBN: 978-1-882330-27-0

ABOUT THE AUTHOR:
Dr. Frederic B. Tate

Frederic grew up in the Appalachian Mountains on the border of Virginia and Tennessee . He graduated from King College with degrees in psychology and art. He earned his masters in psychology from East Tennessee State University and a clinical affiliation in art therapy from Essex County Medical Center . Frederic attended Southern Illinois University for his doctorate and researched graphic symbols of death from Paleolithic to contemporary times for his dissertation. Though his interest in death and dying started much earlier, it was here that he first worked in hospice.

Frederic has published numerous articles on the topic of death and dying and studied with Elizabeth Kübler-Ross when she lived in Virginia . He was one of the founders of Jack's House, a hospice in Tidewater. Currently he works in the psychology department at Eastern State Hospital in Williamsburg , the nation's oldest, public psychiatric hospital. He has worked in the field of hospice for over twenty-five years and in his work often quotes Joan Halifax, "We cannot know death except by dying. This is the mystery that lies beneath the skin of life. But we can feel something from those who are close to it."

This book is dedicated to Gail Robinson Tate,
my favorite sister-in-law.

"My best teachers have been those who were dying. It is through them that I have learned to live."

Dr. Frederic B. Tate

Acknowledgements:

Thank you to Dave, Edna, and Roger for your help and support. Also, a special thank you to Evan for believing in the importance of this book.

Table Of Contents

One:

Initial Thoughts

Life's painful trials and tribulations are necessary and are, in part, what gives fullness and meaning to our existence. My greatest growth has resulted from the times in my life when I hurt the most—the death of a loved one, or a broken heart.

I just wish we were better able to see that death is inevitable and a part of life. It might make living a bit easier for more people. Death can be the end of pain and the ultimate release. For someone who has lived a long life it might be the cessation of emotional suffering and physical constrictions. More often than not, I believe that our society sees death as something that is fearful and negative. Though I have seen progress, our medical profession still sees death as a failure. We teach medical students how to save a life but do not teach them when it is inhumane to keep someone alive. Death is that skeleton in the black robe stalking us. My hope is that this book will, in some small way, help to change this.

Centuries ago it was not uncommon for monks to keep a human skull by their bed or even to sleep in their own coffins.

This served as a reminder that our time here is limited. Though I do not propose something this extreme, I do know that if we acknowledge death and incorporate it into life instead of avoiding it, we might be less afraid of it and life might hold more meaning.

Once I was giving a presentation to a group where I mentioned that in contemporary, Western civilization we tend to eschew death. A participant raised his hand and noted that death was constantly in the media and, in fact, had even encroached into cartoons for children. His point was valid and well taken but I am not referring to the violent deaths depicted in movies and on television. I am addressing rather natural death, old age, illness, etc. I feel that the dehumanization that we too often experience in medical hospitals and the trend toward sending condolences on-line support my supposition. It has become increasingly easy for us to deny death and, in my opinion, we are paying a price for this. Hospice affords a wonderful exception to this rule.

It is easier for us to avoid death than in the past. For the first time in the history of humankind we have a death-free generation of adults. There are many adults who not only have both parents alive but their grandparents are also living. This is a new phenomenon. A year or so ago I was working with a group of young, medical students. Not one of them had experienced the death of a loved one. One student had a fish that died when he was a child but that was it! Not surprisingly, during several of our hypothetical scenarios about working with patients who are dying, they made their decisions based on what was most likely to prevent the possibility of litigation as opposed to the needs and wishes of the patient. At times compassion and empathy are more difficult to find in individuals who have not grieved or suffered. A broken heart tends to make us more human or multi-dimensional. I know that is a generalization but one that I find holds some truth.

When I was young it was easy for me to see the world in black and white. As I have aged I see a lot of gray and very few issues that are simply clear cut. This is especially so when it comes to facing death. The older we get the less we should know and the more comfortable we should be with not knowing. With experience and maturity comes the realization that most of life falls into that gray area and that this is not such a bad thing after all. I was actually a bit disappointed when satellites were first sent to the dark side of the moon. I liked the idea, at least metaphorically, of the moon having some mystery and being partially unexplored.

Twenty five years ago if you had asked me if I believed in reincarnation or guardian angels I would have most likely said no. Now if you were to ask me I would respond, "I do not disbelieve." It is more than mere semantics; there is a world of difference between not believing and not disbelieving. A quarter of a century of hospice experience has most certainly opened my eyes to the more mystical aspects of living and dying. And I have seen my share of phenomena, for a lack of a better word, that I am unable to explain. Some of these are discussed later in the book.

I have several reasons for writing a book on death and dying. Over the years I have continually observed well-meaning people say really insensitive things. I have been guilty of it myself. I remember years ago when I was a little less experienced, walking into a hospital room where the man I had come to visit was dying of AIDS. He was about ninety pounds, covered with skin cancer, and was the same shade of green as the wicked witch in the *Wizard of Oz*. The first thing out of my mouth was "How are you feeling?" I regretted the idiotic question as soon as it came out of my mouth. I asked him if I could start the conversation over. We both laughed. Like most, my intentions were very good, but my mouth opened without the benefit of first engaging my brain. Actually I should have engaged my heart. If I had, I would have been aware that my question simply covered my fear and sadness.

People are not often intentionally cruel when someone has died. It is just that we are not taught what to say and the painful emotions often get in the way. Surprisingly, doctors and ministers are often the worst at talking about death. Physicians are not usually bad or callous people and most of them want to talk with their patients who are dying but they do not know how. If you view death as a failure, it makes it even more difficult. One would think that a chaplain, minister, priest, or rabbi, would automatically be skilled at talking about death, and certainly some are. Some of the most insensitive remarks and actions that I have ever witnessed, however, have come from clergy.

Once I heard a minister tell a mother who had just buried her child that she was fortunate she had another child. Yes, other children may help with the process of grieving but even if a mother has twelve children she is no less devastated when one dies. I also overheard a chaplain tell a dying man that he had to "...be strong and hang on for the sake of his family." I was reminded how much I needed to write a book about communicating with those who are dying. What finally got me to sit and start typing was the young man who told me that he was avoiding a friend with terminal cancer because he simply did not know what to say. How sad for both of them. If this book results in making dying a bit easier for just one person I will consider it successful.

I believe that I am qualified to write this book not so much because of my education but as a result of my experience. I do practice as a psychotherapist and have a doctorate of which I am actually proud—I worked long and hard for my degrees. However, a doctorate makes one educated, not necessarily smart or compassionate. Some of the most unenlightened people I have known have initials after their names. As I have aged I define myself less by my title and profession. What I want to share with the reader does not come from reading text books but from sitting and holding the hands of people as they die. My best teachers have been people who were dying. It is through them that I have learned to live. I have worked with children and adults, people with terminal and life-threatening illnesses, those who were clinically dead and revived, and as a volunteer for hospice. Most importantly, I have buried people I love, friends and family. My friend, Carl, died from lung cancer just a few months ago.

This will help me stay in the heart and out of the head as I write. It is that knowledge and information that I have a need to share with others. My hope is that the reader will be better prepared to talk to those who are dying, to the family, and to friends left with broken hearts.

You will not find a lot of philosophy or scientific research in the following chapters. What I will share really is very simple. I do believe that I am able to make the topics of grieving (emotions) and mourning (the public expression of emotions) a bit more palatable for the average individual. If we can be less fearful in talking about death we are likely to be more compassionate. If we can listen in a nonjudgmental way when someone tells us about a near death experience or refrain from discrediting grief that is the result of a pet's death, we will have made tremendous progress.

Now having said all this, it is important to remind the reader that I do not hold a monopoly on truth and there is no one, right way in a world of individuals to cope with death. When I come across those who claim to know the truth I tend to run in the opposite direction. Even with simple and practical suggestions, talking about death is still difficult. This is not likely to change.

Two:

Why the Field of Death and Dying?

I did not consciously start my career in psychology thinking of working with people who were dying. But fate, the universe, god, however you view it, often puts us where we need to be. As I have aged I believe less and less in accidents.

I grew up in Southwestern Virginia where the mountain laurel grows as tall as trees and in the fall the hills are a blaze of color as far as the eye can see. Though in the fifties it was an area filled with incredible prejudice and superstition, the Appalachian Mountains were an idyllic environment for playing and growing. The first experience I had with death was when I was a child of four. I had an uncle who was driving in the rain from North Carolina to Tennessee. The mountainous roads were dangerous in those days even under the most ideal of conditions. He was instantly killed when he ran head-on into a large truck coming around one of the mountain's curves. I was sleeping and sat up in bed. He was at the foot of the bed and I still remember how fascinated I was because he was translucent and energy was flowing around his body. He told me that he just wanted to say goodbye and let me know that everything was OK. I went back to sleep. In the morning I waked and walked out to the kitchen where both of my sleep-deprived parents were sitting with their ubiquitous coffee and cigarettes. They said that they had some sad news for me. I told them that I already knew and that my uncle was dead and that he had visited me. I remember that my poor father actually got mad. He was most likely an alcoholic even prior to my birth. Until he was in his eighties rage was about the only emotion he was comfortable expressing. I am sure he was frightened by something he could not rationally explain. But at age four I added visitation by the dead to my list of things I should not discuss with my parents. I often wonder if it would have made a difference if they had accepted the experience as natural and encouraged it.

Just the other day I was on the phone with Darrlyn who had been sitting for her four-year-old grandson. On her coffee table was a book of photographs sent back to earth from space craft. He was on the floor quietly flipping through the book. At one point he stopped, gasped, pointed to a picture and named some obscure galaxy. His grandmother went to the book's index and to her astonishment the child had correctly identified this galaxy. He informed her, "See this planet here, that is where I lived before I was planted in Mommy's tummy." Instead of ignoring it or admonishing the little boy for fabricating, she sat beside him and said, "Please tell me all about it. What do you remember?" Even if we do not believe in life after death, even if we do not believe in reincarnation, this is how we should respond to children: openly, nonjudgmentally, and by encouraging dialogue.

I also remember as a small child going into the old, Methodist church that was in our neighborhood. I was riding my tricycle in the church parking lot. The door to the church was open so using a five year old's logic I rode the bike into the church. I noticed a casket on the alter. I drove up to it and there was a lady in it who appeared to be ancient. At five, though, anyone over thirty is ancient. I got off my bike and went up to the alter to look at her. She looked like she was sleeping. I touched her and remember shaking her to see if she was merely sleeping. I had no fear at all, just curiosity. Once I determined that she was really dead I hopped back on the bike and rode out of the sanctuary. My guess is that I left little fingerprints all over the undertaker's carefully applied make-up.

When I was in high school I had a friend die in an auto accident and a neighbor who died of a heart attack. But it was not until college with the death of my German grandmother, that I experienced the death of someone I truly loved. Though I did not have the same experience I had when my uncle died, I walked into my dorm room and I knew my grandmother had died. It was filled with her perfume—an old-fashion smell of violets and lilly of the valley. Interestingly, my aunt had the exact same experience at the same time. But it was not until years later that I discovered this. Most of us have at least heard of stories of loved ones visiting when they die, even if we have not personally experienced it.

My friend, Olivia, was talking with her sister who was dying of breast cancer. She asked Olivia what sign she would like to receive as a message that she was OK after she died. Olivia thought about it and asked for a rainbow. She was beside her sister when she died. After a while she left the room and in passing a relative who had been out on the porch said, "You would not believe the beautiful rainbow that is in the sky." Olivia had forgotten about the promise but ran outside immediately to see the rainbow.

When I went to Illinois for my doctorate it was the early 80's and the new "gay cancer", as AIDS was called at that time, had started to kill young, gay men. My faculty advisor, Harry, was working in hospice. As a result of his work and research I started moving in that direction. It was at the same time that my friend, Brent, became ill. He had a cold that he was unable to shake. Brent was bisexual and even by my liberal standards, very promiscuous. It got worse and he ended up in the ICU in Springfield diagnosed with pneumonia. He was in isolation and was dead within a few days. Samples from his autopsy were sent to the Center for Disease Control in Atlanta and it was confirmed that he was one of the first in the state to die from this new Gay Related Immunosuppressant Disease. It was even before AIDS was confirmed to be a virus.

I can understand that he was in isolation; the medical team did not know what they were dealing with. I am sure they feared it could be an airborne illness. But he died with no skin-to-skin contact, no preparation, no opportunity to say goodbye, and totally isolated. Friends and family were not allowed in. A few days after his death, I saw his possessions, as then recommended by the health department, taken from his apartment, placed in the dumpster, and burned. I wanted just to salvage a book or something to remember my friend.

I know it sounds a little melodramatic, somewhat like Scarlet O'Hara on her knees in the dirt digging for food shouting "As god is my witness…." But I did watch the burning of Brent's worldly possessions and promised that if I could make dying a little easier for just one person, I would do it. I have kept my promise and hope that there are many people who would say that I have helped others live until they die.

Three:

Elizabeth Kübler-Ross

When I finished my doctorate I moved from Illinois to Iowa, having taken a position working with Native Americans in the field of substance abuse. It was soon after moving there that my mother died. A week after my mother's death my dear friend and professor, Walter Brown, also died. It was under his tutelage in New Jersey that I had earned clinical affiliation in art therapy. If there is any one form of communication and therapy that has served me well working with people with terminal and life-threatening illnesses, it is art therapy. At times, words just get in the way and art offers a form of expression that is universal and easily taps into the rich area of the subconscious. When my mother died I was isolated and went through most of the process of mourning alone. My grief was compounded by the fact that I was experiencing the death of two people I loved.

Elizabeth Kübler-Ross was living in Head Waters, Virginia at that time and still in good health. I sent her a letter stating that I needed to come to Virginia and work with her. I told her of my limited finances and student loans, offering to work at her facility in turn for the opportunity to spend time with her. She wrote back and said in typical Kübler-Ross fashion, "Just come. Pay what you can." I took her a copy of my dissertation which was on death symbols and imagery as a gift of appreciation. Her ideas greatly influenced my writing and her warm words touched my heart.

It was October and the fall color in the mountains was beautiful. I was sitting alone in the woods prior to my first session with Elizabeth. All of a sudden an enormous stag burst through the trees and stood right in front of me. At first I was frightened because he was so large and I thought he might charge. He stared at me for a few seconds and then fell over right at my feet. An arrow was protruding out of his side. It was then that I heard the hunters coming thought the woods. I reached over to touch the deer, his breathing was shallow and he did not try to move. I left because I could not face what would happen when the hunters reached the animal. A devotee of CG Jung and his concept of synchronicity, I immediately found symbolism in the experience. I was in the right place; I needed to mourn.

I have fond memories of Elizabeth and consider her to be the mother of the hospice movement in this country. I still recommend her book *On Death and Dying*. She is no longer in vogue and some authors now talk a bit despairingly about her. I am not a Freudian therapist by any means and agree with few of

Freud's theories. However, he was the foundation on which my profession was established and it would be easy to criticize him by today's standards. We do not need to put someone's light out to make ours shine brighter.

Elizabeth talked about the stages of dying including shock, denial, anger, bargaining, and resolution. Today the research favors the tasks of grieving. I agree that this makes sense but we do not need to toss the baby out with the bathwater. The ironic thing is that during one conversation I had with Elizabeth she told me that she wished that she had never presented the stages of death and dying. She said that they were never meant to be firm stages set in stone. "Americans," she said, "are so eager to categorize and simplify that the stages were totally misconstrued." She intended for them be a general guide for observing reactions and was the first to admit that people skip stages and that they are not always universal. You do not look at your watch and say to someone who is dying, "You have been in shock now for a good thirty minutes. Maybe it is time to move on to denial." Paradigms come and go, and they all have validity.

I find her stages very helpful and have observed that not only do people who are dying go though stages but so do those of us left behind to grieve. When someone first receives a diagnosis of cancer, when parents are told their infant is mentally retarded, or when a spouse or lover is unfaithful, people tend to experience many of the same stages. After all, each of the above situations is a type of loss.

The state of denial seems to cause the most difficulty for practitioners. Not many people die in denial. We usually die the way we have lived. If someone used denial as a coping mechanism throughout their life they are likely to use it when they are dying. I have seen less experienced students and caregivers attack denial as if armed with a chisel and hammer. I had a very astute professor say to me once that it was best not to remove denial unless we were certain that the client had something with which to replace it.

Take away denial and you might have a suicidal client. I have learned that you can rarely break through denial anyway, and to try to do so is cruel and unnecessary. Some people die in denial. That is their lesson. It is OK. We are to sit compassionately with their denial and be available in case it does change.

I remember a woman once who was dying of liver cirrhosis secondary to years of chronic alcohol addiction. She was jaundiced, the color of a pumpkin. Her abdomen was distended as if she were in the final trimester of pregnancy. It is difficult to be in denial with that type of overt, physical evidence. When they determined that she was dying I went into her room to talk with her. I told her what the physicians were saying and asked her how she felt about it. She smiled and told me that all the labs and medical reports were in error, that she was just pregnant and would be fine. I never brought up the topic of death again but came to her room daily and sat with her and talked. She died a month or so later, totally in denial until the end. The difficult part was dealing with the countertransferrance of staff and convincing them that it made no difference if she was in denial or not.

Now there are situations where denial could have an outcome that is potentially harmful. For example, if this woman had a family member who she refused to contact because she believed that she would deliver the baby and be fine. Her denial could rob that family member of an opportunity to help and to say good bye. In a situation like that I would have worked around the denial as best I could, attempting to get permission to contact family. It sometimes takes creativity and patience.

Author Alan Wolfelt who writes and lectures on the topic of death and dying does not use the term "closure" but talks about "reconciliation". He presents tasks of grieving as opposed to stages. I agree that reconciliation is a better word. Wolfelt states that the death of someone loved changes our lives forever and that our task is to journey through the grief, not to avoid it. The journey toward reconciliation requires acknowledging the reality of the death. As those of us who have experienced loss know, this is much easier said than done. In my experience it is not unusual for someone to accept the reality of the death one day, only to move back into denial the next. This is normal. Remember, though there are many shared aspects of mourning, the journey is unique for each of us.

According to Wolfelt, other tasks include embracing the pain of the loss. He is not saying that you should not distract yourself from the pain of death at times, but that when we are feeling stronger and safer, we need to move back toward the pain. When we live in a society that wants us to "stay strong" or "keep our chin up" and return to work fully functioning after three days, it is an extra challenge to move into the pain of grief. The message we get is to repress rather than express our grief. I have often felt that our society does a good job of responding to grief initially in the acute phase, but we fail miserably in the long term.

Mourning takes as long as it takes. It is best not to set a timetable for mourning. As Ellen Goodman, columnist with the *Boston Globe* said, "This vocabulary of closure has spread across the post-modern landscape like a nail across my blackboard. It comes with an intonation of sympathy but an accent of impatience." In real life grief is a train that does not run on anyone else's schedule. The expectation of closure and healing is nothing but an added burden. We create a sense of failure. It is not good to set timelines because we are each different.

Though most of us never totally "recover" from, or achieve complete "closure" following a death, there are indications that one is adapting to a death. Wolfelt and other authors believe there are several indicators that a person is forming a healthy adaptation to a death. Acknowledging and feeling the reality of the death, resuming roles (jobs, parenting, etc.), feeling that the pain of grief is becoming less overwhelming, finding pleasure in life again, resuming meaningful connections with others, and maintaining a connection with the deceased, are some of the primary indicators.

I do not believe that we ever achieve closure or get over the death of a loved one. Even if it were possible, I am not sure it would be a good thing. I no longer have the agonizing, empty pain I had the first few weeks after my mother's death. However, even after a quarter of a century without her I have a bittersweet sadness when I think of her. I would not want to loose this feeling. To tell someone that the journey will end when they have recovered from grief is not true and not helpful. We can adjust and adapt. Though loss may never disappear, it does soften. Adaptation is knowing that we can live and move forward, even with a broken heart. It is finding joy and meaning in life even after the death of someone we love.

Four:

The Philosophy of Hospice

The word "hospice" comes from the shelters that were built for travelers and pilgrims going to the Holy Lands in the Middle Ages. The first modern hospice was founded in London in 1968. A few years ago I was hiking through the southwest tip of Ireland exploring Neolithic stone circles. There were hospices in that part of the world as early as 800 AD but the structures no longer exist. At that time people with leprosy were often fed by the nuns and monks who ran the hospices. In 1974 the first American hospice was started in Connecticut. Interestingly, the hospice movement has been significantly less successful in China, Korea, and Japan. There is still a cultural taboo in many Asian countries against talking about someone's personal, medical condition. The writings of Elizabeth Kübler-Ross were instrumental to the development of this new philosophy of care for individuals who were dying.

Most of us, though not all of us, prefer, if possible, to spend our last days at home with the people we love. The hospice movement is dedicated to making this happen. Hospice is an end-of-life care that allows the individual to die at home, or in a setting that is home-like. The primary goal is to keep the patient free of pain and to incorporate emotional and spiritual needs as well as medical. Hospice and palliative care aim to help the person live until they die. Hospice workers understand that the quality of life is more important than the quantity. Though nothing is done to end life, nothing is done to prevent the individual from dying. Care for, and support of the family member, is also paramount.

For most hospice programs the patient needs to be diagnosed with a terminal condition with a life expectancy of six months or less. If the person's condition improves or there is a remission, they are discharged from hospice and can return to aggressive therapy or go on about their daily life. They can return to hospice in the future if such is needed.

Palliative care is the active, total care of people whose disease is not responsive to curative treatment. Hospice and palliative care affirm life and regard dying as a normal process. Surgery and chemotherapy can have a place in palliative care, provided that their benefits clearly outweigh the disadvantages.

Pain control is only one aspect of hospice. Hospice is also there to offer a calm passage through the journey of fear, despair, and loss of control. This requires careful listening and communicating with those who are dying. These interactions can, at times, be cryptic. Hospice offers an environment of non-abandonment and empowerment. Toward the end of life empowerment may be as simple as giving the dying individual a choice between having the shades of the window up or down, or picking between two types of tea. Hospice workers know that adequate pain management is less likely to happen if a person feels abandoned or discredited.

Hospice nurses and volunteers are a rare and wonderful breed. As a collective they are much more open to more nontraditional methods of treatment such as massage, therapeutic touch, energy work, acupressure, pet therapy, and art therapy. There is research indicating that physicians who work in palliative care and hospice tend to get the highest ratings for a good bed-side manner. The best way for any physician to be liked by patients and family is to turn the pager off, sit beside the patient, to praise the caregivers, and be sure to touch the patient before leaving the room. It is that simple.

This information comes from interviews with people who were dying and from the family members who were caring for them. Again, our knowledge and skills are important, but I cannot overstate the importance of touch when working with people who are terminally ill. Touch is healing. In this case I am not using the word to mean healing in a sense of curing a disease, but in calming the heart and soul.

Five:

Experiencing Death

When I was in graduate school I saw the movie *Fanny and Alexander* by Ingmar Bergman. There is a scene in which the father dies. The mother paces back and forth in front of the casket clinching her fists and moaning. I had experienced death by this time in my life. Though I loved my grandmother dearly and was saddened when she died, it was not a tragedy. It was not until my mother's death years later that for the first time I realized how realistic the movie's depiction of death was. Bergman, I think, would have had to experience death to have produced that scene.

My mother committed suicide right before Thanksgiving. It was not until several years later, however, that I learned it was a suicide. The evidence was clear but I was unable to see it initially due to grief, shock, and, no doubt, some denial. She called both my brother and me. Though she and I talked every Sunday evening, it was not a Sunday. That alone should have been a warning but again, I did not pick up on it until after the fact. Only a few hours after I talked with her I received a call from my aunt. My father had come home and found her dead most likely from an overdose of sleeping pills. He called his sister and she came to the house and had the difficult job of calling my brother and me. I remember the feeling of disbelief and panic, and the horrible agony once the reality hit. I lay on the floor in a fetal position for what must have been hours. Somehow I managed to sleep a few hours that evening. It was devastating when I sat up in bed and realized it had not been a dream. Fortunately my friend Suz put some food in me, helped me pack, and drove me to the airport.

Thank god for Suz. When someone is in shock, asking what we can do to help is useless. We may have to temporarily take charge and find specific things to do and assign tasks even if it washing dishes or polishing dress shoes for the funeral.

I went through the funeral doing what needed to be done. I was happy to get back to work when the funeral was over to distract myself. When I walked up to my apartment I noticed a box at the door. It was a package that my mother had sent to me a day or so before her death. I saw her handwriting and just sat on the porch and cried. I knew that I was not going to be able to escape the pain as easily as I thought. There was going to be no vacation from this hurt. Having worked in hospice while studying for my doctorate did not lessen the pain, but I at least understood that what I was feeling was perfectly normal, and I was able to be very gentle with myself. I did return to Virginia for the holidays because I felt my father and brother needed me there. My father's story was that she had died of a heart attack. I never challenged that even when I knew it was not true. It did not matter. I do not think he was able to face the fact that it was a suicide and that his drinking may have been, in part, a cause of her unhappiness.

Decorating the Christmas tree with my mother's ornaments, many of which she brought over from Germany with her, was one of the most painful things I have ever done. Christmas had so many wonderful memories. Six months was a magic number for me. It was about this time that the dark hole of agony in my chest decreased. The pain lessened and became more bearable. It was two steps forward and one back, but I was still progressing. It took a long time for the reality of the fact that I would not ever be able to sit over a cup of coffee and talk with her again to register. I do enjoy Thanksgiving and Christmas. But they have never been the same and never will be.

Grief is such a strange creature with its own agenda. I had several months where my crying was under control and I was returning to my premorbid self. I was shopping in a grocery store. I saw a jar of pickled herring. I hate herring in any form but my mother loved them. She would sit with a fork and eat them right out of the jar. I burst into tears and had to leave the store and sit in my car for fifteen minutes until I regained control. Grief can sneak up on us when we least expect it. My friend, Karen, lost her brother to cancer a month ago. She was at the mall a few weeks after his death and saw a young brother and sister holding hands. Karen told me she had to leave the mall. I understood what she was feeling.

It has been about twenty five years now since my mother's death. When I think of my mother it is a bitter-sweet feeling, the extreme grief passed quickly. I knew my mother had some depression but none of us knew to what extent. Initially I asked myself what if I had done something differently. But "what ifs" will drive you crazy if you spend too much time with them.

Part of my work has been sitting with people as they review their "what ifs" and regrets. People can really beat themselves up with guilt. There have been times when people made unfortunate decisions that resulted in a death. I listen non-judgmental but do not rush to make it OK.

I was talking with a group of Emergency Medical Technicians from Richmond a while back. They had responded to a call and when they got to the house the mother was at the door with her child in her arms—he was obviously dead. They took the child into the ambulance and did everything they could to revive him but were unsuccessful. Because the mother saw this she will be faced with fewer "what ifs". Often hospitals move family out of the room when there is a code. The excuse is that they get in the way but I think the unexpressed reason is often fear of litigation. But if the family observes medical staff attempting to save a life, their grief is less likely to be complicated.

What helped me the most during the first year following my mother's death were the friends who called and sent cards each week and who would ask me about how I was doing when they called. For me, talking about it and my feelings were very helpful. The time I spent with Elizabeth Kübler-Ross was also tremendously healing. There were people at the center who were dying and those, like me, who had experienced a death. Sitting with a mother who just lost a child or a father who watched helplessly as his son fell to his death, helped me put my pain in perspective. It was comforting for me to be around other people who were mourning. I actually got to a point where I could no longer cry—but this was good. I still keep in touch with Susan, now living in New Mexico, whom I met so many years ago at that center. People tend to bond strongly and quickly in that type of atmosphere where emotions are so open. Sadly, experiences like this are considered artificial. It is true but I find it sad that supportive, emotional environments are so rare that people have to be warned and brought back "down to earth" prior to leaving.

I remember Elizabeth telling me that I had to be sure to do my own work. I gravitate toward people in need and they tend to find me. This is good but at this time I had to do my own mourning and not concentrate on helping others. She wisely reminded me that my grief was no more or less than the grief of anyone else and that I needed to focus on myself.

I shared a room with three other guys when I was at the center. One was dying from cancer, one from AIDS, and one from brain tumors secondary to the Agent Orange that he was exposed to in Vietnam. AIDS was still new and some people were uncomfortable being around those who had it. The man had a seizure several days into the workshop and did not return—he died a few weeks later. I made sure to sit with him at meals because there was such an incredible stigma attached to AIDS at this time. The people there battling cancer were seen as heroic, but not the people dying from AIDS. I communicated with the man with the brain tumors for a few months after the conference—he died a year or so later. At this time the military was still denying any connection between the chemicals and the tumors and he had no funding or medical reimbursement from them. He had to deal with the fact that he was dying and the anger from being denied medical care and support.

It was interesting living with three people who were dying. I remember waking up about three in the morning and they were sitting drinking tea and talking. I asked them why there were not sleeping. One responded, "Soon we will have eternal sleep. We want to talk while we can." I understood.

Everyone who is dying should be given at least one opportunity to talk about death. It is a bit incomprehensible but people can go three years with a diagnosis of a terminal illness, spend months in and out of the hospital, and still not be given the opportunity to talk about death. It is a myth that if someone does not ask about their condition they do not want to talk about it. I use the image of knocking on a door. When I am working with someone who is dying I always make at least one attempt to talk about death. If they do not want to talk about it, and this does happen but rarely, I honor it. I do not have the right to repeatedly pound on the door. What people thank me as they approach death is for talking with them about death. Often what I hear is that their family was unable to talk about it. But that does not eliminate the need. We are so fearful of how people will react to bringing up the topic of death. I have never had anyone become hysterical or jump out the window. I have had a few people say that they were not dying and I did not pursue the conversation. That has been my worse case scenario.

It is important that we never lie to someone with a terminal illness. I read a research article once where eighty-five percent of the physicians interviewed said it was OK to lie to or withhold information from someone who is dying. Their justification was to decrease anxiety. Interestingly, only two percent of the patients with a terminal illness who were interviewed said that they did not want their physicians to be totally honest with them about their illness and prognosis. What if you were dying and I knew it, and I chose not to tell you? I might rob you of the opportunity to patch up a relationship or to take that trip to Hawaii you always wanted to take. When we lie we potentially rob people of opportunities. We are not taught how to respond to difficult questions such as "Am I dying," "I am afraid," or "How long do I have to live?" As a result we tend to give hasty, untruthful, unhelpful reassurance.

The art of it all is of course, being honest without removing hope. There is a big difference between saying, "With this type of cancer you will be dead in two months," and "The average life expectancy with the type of cancer you have is around two months. However, there are people who have lived much longer than that and though rare, people who have had remissions and cures. What do you feel is going to happen?" We never have the right to remove hope. I have sat with many people who were dying and for whom I had no doubt that death was only hours or days away. I would never say to someone in this position, "Hang in there. There is hope!" But when asked if there was hope I always responded "Yes." Maybe they would not live, but that does not negate hope for such. When asked, "Am I dying?" I always gently turn the question back to them, "Do you think you are dying?" If they say no, I promise to be beside them as they fight. I personally see death as a "cure" or a "healing." This helps me to be more comfortable when the topic comes up.

Supporting someone who chooses not to give up hope is different from forcing our hope and optimism onto someone who has given up the hope of living. When someone tells me there is no hope of living I promise to support them until they stop living and reassure them it is OK to give up hope. When we encourage people to keep up hope we unintentionally burden them. Giving up hope is not a bad thing—it might simply be that they are resolved to the inevitable. Most often people who are resolved to their death are calm and at peace. Those who do not give up hope are not morally stronger or psychologically healthier than someone who does not have hope. Not everyone can maintain a positive outlook at death nor should they be encouraged to do so.

One practical point in closing this chapter, if you have experienced the death of a loved one be sure to have a complete physical in a year. Mourning is hard work and it does lower the immune system. There is a strong, positive correlation between illnesses within several years of having experienced a death. After a death we need to walk and rest, even though it is the last thing we feel like doing. It is also important in my experience that people who are grieving increase fluids and avoid alcohol.

Six:

Medicating Grief

I am by no means opposed to medication. There are times following a death when medication is warranted. If someone has not been sleeping for an extended period of time (more than one or two nights) they would most certainly benefit from a sleeping pill. Sleep deprivation is a horrible feeling and will only intensify and interfere with the process of mourning. Understandably, the use of a sleeping aid should be discontinued as soon as possible. There are times when antidepressants and anti-anxiety agents should be used. For example, if someone who is grieving has a premorbid history of suicide or depression they may need medication to help them through a difficult time. Medication can help stabilize someone in crisis and even save lives. Grief is overwhelming and intense for any of us, but for someone with a fragile psychological composition it can be dangerous. Medication may help them get through the dangerous period so they can address the grief, but by bit, when they are stronger. Anyone who is an imminent danger to themselves or others should be considered for treatment and medication.

If you are over fifty you will clearly remember the image of the veiled Jacqueline Kennedy walking behind her husband's casket. Biographers said that she was heavily sedated during the funeral. I do not mention this to judge the first lady. I have experienced the death of a loved one but I was allowed to mourn privately—I did not have the entire world watching me. But I wonder when the expression of grief started to be seen as a weakness or as undignified. The image of the stoic, stiff upper lip, is nothing new but has somehow become the expectation in our culture as the appropriate way to publically express (or not express!) our grief.

It is rare but some individuals will need psychiatric hospitalization secondary to a death. Having a strong support system and a history of successfully dealing with crises decrease the probability of this happening. I think all of us should talk to a counselor, therapist, or join a bereavement support group following the death of a loved one, even if only for a few sessions. But it is hard for me to be objective about therapy. Most of us will at least briefly, meet the criteria for clinical depression when we are grieving. I wish talking to a therapist during or after the death of a loved one was as standard as going to a dentist when we have a tooth ache. I know that this is not realistic. Many people cannot afford a therapist and others fear the stigma attached to seeking psychological help. And again many of us, mostly men, see asking for emotional support as a weakness. I have had friends in the military who said they wanted psychological support during and after the death of a family member and that such help was even available. However, they had commanding officers who they felt would see it as a sign of weakness and that it could actually hinder future promotions. In one case my friend in the navy paid out-of-pocket for a therapist so that the military would have no record of such.

Having stated that I am not opposed to medication, it is important that I say that we too often medicate grief. Mourning is painful and we do not like pain. In this society where we turn to medication to immediately relieve all discomfort, we are quick to ask for and to obtain medications. When someone we love dies we are supposed to hurt. The list of physical and psychological symptoms is numerous: anxiety, depression, loss of appetite, confusion, shock, insomnia, heart palpitations, panic attacks, and restlessness. These are normal feelings during grief. Again, we hurt when our heart is broken. We are supposed to hurt. Covering up the hurt with medication in a cavalier fashion is not always helpful. Sitting with our discomfort is never easy or pleasant. But it is exactly what we need to do.

Those working in the field of hospice know that the number one fear for people who are dying is not death. It is pain and a loss of independence. Our archaic attitudes toward medicating individuals who are terminally ill are slowly starting to change. My impression over the years is that we tend to over-medicate individuals who are grieving but too often under-medicate those who are dying. I credit the hospice movement with this much needed shift in paradigms. Sadly, it seems that the prime motivator in getting those who are dying proper pain control is as a result of recent litigation. For the first time physicians and facilities are being successfully sued by family members who saw loved ones die in pain because they were insufficiently medicated. But as long as individuals in hospice have their pain controlled, I am less concerned as to how or why.

I think it is criminal how difficult it is for those with terminal and life-threatening illnesses to get prescriptions for cannabis. It can significantly decrease pain and anorexia. But it might be best that I do not get on this soap-box. One of my favorite memories from working in the AIDS hospice was when I took lunch into one of the clients. Two nuns who volunteered there were in the room talking with him. He was sitting up in bed smoking a joint and over his bed was a calendar filled with gay pornography. Mr. July had on a cowboy hat and boots and nothing else. The nuns, who were two of the most compassionate people I had ever met, were sitting among the pot smoke and porn and never batted an eye! They sat with anyone of any denomination and never preached or judged.

I am not sure how many times over the years have I seen people needlessly die in pain but it has been more than the reader would believe possible. Watching someone start to moan and scream at three hours after their last dose of medication and being told by the medical staff that the next pill was not due until four hours from the last dose is torture. The good news is that it occurs less often and if the individual is in hospice, it does not occur at all.

It is not something that I can prove in any empirical way but I do believe that I have not only seen people needlessly die in pain, but needlessly die. With their white lab coats and stethoscopes, physicians can be modern versions of the voodoo witch doctor. If a physician says to a patient who happens to be more passive "You have two months to live," they might actually die in two months just to be a compliant patient! We laugh at the movies where a witch doctor points a bone at someone and curses them. But we underestimate that the words of a physician can be equally harmful.

People should never die in pain. There are times when extreme measures have to be taken. For example, an anesthesiologist may need to be called in. I remember one case in which a man's pain from his bone cancer became unbearable. The physician agreed to put him to sleep, promising to wake him when his daughter arrived from across the country with the new grandchild he wanted to see. When she arrived he was waked, spent as much time as he could with his family, and then was again put to sleep. It was a wonderful example of honoring the individual's wishes and keeping the promise of controlling their pain.

Inadequate pain medication happens for several reasons. Physicians have strict regulations in some states and fear litigation. Others are improperly trained—not knowing the difference between addiction and tolerance. Just a few months ago I actually heard a physician say "We can't give her morphine. That is the big gun and we need to save it." Morphine may or may not be the big gun, it depends on the individual and the nature of the pain, and even if it was the big gun it should not be held for later.

Pain control is not easy. It often takes times to find the right medications and the therapeutic dose and it continuously needs to be reevaluated. There is a strong psychological component to pain also. If someone is anxious their perceived pain will be greater. A good nurse knows this and looks at psyche and soma, mind and body, when addressing pain. The emotions affect the body and our physical condition affects the mind. Both need to be addressed.

There are, too, times when people are offered sufficient amounts of pain medication and refuse it. Again, I have witnessed this more often with men than women. Our society has pushed the ridiculous notion that tolerating pain is an indication of moral fortitude. Never should pain be a mark of courage. In my experience, this is more often an issue with the individual dying, not the family. Working gently but persistently with these people, reminding them that proper pain control will add to the quality of life, usually results in a change of attitude.

I mentioned in the first chapter that my friend, Carl, died of lung cancer as I was working on this book. Though his sons and girlfriend were sad when he died and we all miss him terribly, his death really was beautiful. Even though he died in the hospital the system actually got it right. In part, this was because I was there and attempted to serve as an advocate for his needs. The medical staff were adequate, but he sure did not receive the quality of care he would have had with hospice. The last three days of Carl's life we managed to keep his discomfort at a minimum without totally knocking him out. The hardest part for me was watching him struggle with his breathing even with the assistance of oxygen. His lungs by this point were just too damaged to absorb what his body needed.

Both of his sons were at his bedside and we waited for Claire to drive up from South Carolina. He recognized her when she came in and I gave them several hours to just be with him and hold his hand. As I had promised Carl, I asked the nurse to call the physician and request morphine. This was started in the IV drip and about twenty minutes later he stopped breathing. The people around the bedside had not even noticed. I told them that this was as far as we could go with Carl on this journey and left the room so they could be alone. After completing some paperwork and packing his personal possessions, they left. I asked permission to say behind and wash Carl's body and spend some time alone with him. The nursing staff told me I could have as much time as I needed. I washed my friend's fragile shell of a body and just sat with him for a while. It was really very peaceful.

Seven:

Death of a Spouse

In this chapter I will use the word spouse for consistency. I define spouse, however, simply as a partner with whom one has lived. Married, unmarried, gay, straight, one month or seventy years—it is all immaterial.   A legal marriage of forty years does not automatically mean greater love or greater grief when one of the partners dies. As I have stated before, grief is grief.

For most of us losing a spouse is devastating but it is important, first, to address the fact that this is not always the case and we should not automatically assume such. Each time I go to talk with someone who has experienced a death I try to leave expectations at the door. I remember one widow who was positively energized at her husband's funeral. Her smiles and laughter were more in keeping with a cocktail party than what we usually see at a funeral. Was she mourning? Was she heartbroken? Most definitely. She told me that she had lost her husband, her soul mate, her best friend. Those who knew this lady well were aware that her happiness was not a result of her husband's death but that he was no longer suffering. He had been a prisoner in his deteriorating body for over a year and his life was almost void of quality. The human heart is amazing—we are capable of mourning the death of a spouse and at the same time be joyous and thankful that suffering has come to an end.

There have been times too, when I have worked with women who were abused, sometimes physically and sometimes psychologically, by their spouses. Though an abused woman can still be shattered when her husband dies, there are some women who understandably, feel only relief. I mention these exceptions to the rule because some people are taken aback when a spouse is not mourning in the way that society dictates they should. I have always considered it my obligation to meet the individual where they are and not to judge. If they are absolutely destroyed by the death of a spouse or if they are relieved, that is where I meet them. We may not always know the full history behind why someone is or is not mourning. There are those who might attempt to shame a widow for example, who seems "too happy." This is as unfair as judging someone who is sobbing and needs to be physically carried out of a funeral as being too "weak."

I remember a woman I once worked with in therapy who was married to a very negative and abusive husband. After his death she purged the house of his possessions, painted each room, got a new bed, and smashed his favorite coffee mug, dumped the pieces on his grave, spat on the headstone, and walked away. I actually thought that this was cathartic. It was a ritual of starting over with a clean slate. We were able to start slowly working through her scars in therapy. We need to remember there are exceptions and that they are OK.

In the fields of anthropology and social psychology it has often been assumed that the maternal instinct is always the strongest of all innate drives. We are also told that the death of a child is a mother's greatest fear. But research indicates that this is not always the case. Women, especially those who are totally dependent, financially and emotionally, on their husbands, when given a hypothetical scenario of the death of a child verses the death of the husband, rate the latter as more painful and debilitating. Some readers who are mothers might find this information incomprehensible. What we can learn from this information is that the reaction to the death of a spouse depends on numerous factors and is very individual.

The majority, of course, are shattered when a spouse dies. I am in my fifties and find it humbling to sit with a man who is in his eighties and has just lost his wife of sixty years. They were together as husband and wife longer than I have been alive.

Readers who are my age or older will remember George Burns, the comedian with the ever-present cigar. When his wife and comic side-kick, Gracie Allen, died of cancer in the early sixties, he was grief-stricken and never stopped mourning her death. During one interview he confessed that he slept on her side of the bed because he found it comforting and felt close to her. I have so frequently been moved by the simple, little actions that people take following the death of a spouse to help ease the pain of grief. Once I had a friend who made a stuffed bear out of the favorite shirt of the deceased and gave that as a gift to his wife. I though that was such a wonderful, creative idea.

If you experience the death of a spouse do what you need to do for comfort and do not let well-meaning family and friends pressure you to do otherwise. It is OK to keep his clothing in the closet and his razor in the medicine cabinet. It is OK to sleep on her side of the bed and not remove her unfinished book or knitting. It is OK to still celebrate an anniversary or to purchase his favorite cookies at the grocery store. To do these things has nothing to do with "not accepting" the death or being in denial. It is an initial way of coping with the over-whelming feelings of loss. Often we need to cope one little step at a time.

One thing that I have observed hundreds of times over the years is the surviving spouse saying that going into a quiet, empty house is intolerable. After a death many spouses have radios and televisions going in several rooms. I have one friend who recently rented out a room to a law student because she needs noise and activity back in her house following her boyfriend's death. I was talking with a man the other day— his wife died several months ago. They had a ritual where he came home from work and they would fix a martini and sit and read or talk for an hour before dinner. Predictably, this is the most difficult time of day for him and when he misses her the most. My aunt Evie is the opposite. She tells me that following my uncle's death, coming back to the home is very comforting for her, and even when she is there alone she finds it peaceful. I have, however, worked with mourning spouses who could not wait to move. Being in the same space and all the memories were too intolerable to take. And some of us need activity and people around us as we mourn and others need to do it alone. Again, there is no one, correct way to mourn in a world of individuals.

We do not need to dread anniversary dates. But it is best to be prepared. My heart had always ached for my friend, Cyndi, who has mother's day, her son's birthday, and the anniversary of his death all within a few days of each other. When we lose someone we love it is never easy but anniversary dates (birthdays, holidays, anniversary of the death, etc.) can be difficult. For many of us anniversary dates become less agonizing over time. Some individuals will do well to surround themselves with friends and activities on these special dates to give them support and serve as a much needed distraction. Understanding the importance of ritual, I believe that visiting the grave or having a remembrance service can be comforting. Anniversary dates can also be wonderful opportunities to cry and to mourn, decreasing the probability of complicated or unresolved grief. Granted they can be a painful gift, but a gift nonetheless.

Allow me to switch gears for a moment and talk about something that is more practical than emotional but equally as important. One lesson I learned early on in my hospice work was the importance of having a living will. I have seen enough horror stories resulting from a lack of preparation for dying that I cannot stress the importance of this enough. None of us like to think about the possibility of being the next fatality of an automobile accident or the next cancer diagnosis. I wish everyone who reads this book would get a living will, medical power of attorney, organ donor card, and a folder filled with information (financial statements, bank statements, life insurance policies, keys to safety deposit boxes, emergency contact numbers, copies of wills) and let family and friends know where these are. Attached to my living will there is even a letter addressing that I want to be cremated and my wishes after death. Be sure that all documents are signed, dated, notarized, and witnessed. This is not morbid. It is practical. Not to prepare for the unexpected is really, in my opinion, selfish. We save our loved ones a lot of pain and stress if we are organized and prepared. It does not matter if we are young or if we are healthy.

I am not suggesting that having the financial and practical aspects of death organized will decrease grief. It does not, but what it does is prevent the spouse left behind from making major decisions at a time when they can not even think clearly. We often advise people not to make major decisions about finances or selling a house for the first year after a death. Though having a will in place may not decrease grief, it leaves a spouse better prepared and may exacerbate the pain and stress.

As a collective younger couples are much more likely to share the responsibility of financial management. My experience, especially with women of my parent's generation, has often been eye-opening. I have been surprised at the number of middle aged women who had husbands die unexpectedly and had no knowledge of legal and financial issues. Some could not even say what their spouse's income was or where they banked. Can you imagine the helplessness of the widow who was planning the funeral of her husband who had just died of a heart attack, only to find out that he had withheld the fact that they were close to bankruptcy? If you are a spouse, male or female, who leaves the finances to your partner, please prepare for the unexpected even if the two of your are uncomfortable talking about it. Preventing a fire will be a lot less painful than putting one out.

When my friend Dave's father was diagnoses with pancreatic cancer he immediately went into action. He met with his attorney and made sure his wife would not have to deal with any legal or financial issues when he died. He made Dave the executor and knowing that his one daughter had a track record of manipulating his wife, had a clause placed in the will that any attempt to contest it would result in her forfeiting her inheritance. This is an example, though rare, of fire prevention at its best.

When a partner dies it is unlikely that just the spouse will be affected. There is an enormous Calder mobile suspended from the ceiling of the art museum in Norfolk. If you were to hit one of the metal disks on this movable sculpture, all of the other parts would be set into motion. All are interconnected. So it is when a family member dies. If the wife dies the father may have to take on the role of both mother and father. Children, grandparents, in-laws, all may be affected. This can often make mourning more complex.

With any death, that of a spouse or otherwise, the journey is usually uneven. Initially the survivors will have good moments that eventually turn into good days. So often though, it is one step forward and two back. We may go several days feeling strong with some control over our emotions to be hit the next day with agony as intense as the day of the death. This is normal. But it sure is not easy. Throughout the years I have been asked over and over again by mourning spouses why they are not "progressing" or "healing" faster. I remind them that mourning takes as long as it takes and that their uneven journey is normal.

In the book *Being With Dying*, author Joan Halifax uses the analogy of death being like a ringing phone. We can temporarily silence it through shock, denial, medication, or alcohol. But the ringing continues in the background and eventually, if we are to adapt to our loss, the phone needs to be answered. A good friend will sit with survivors as they answer this call. Initially it may need to be answered over and over again.

Allowing others to comfort us, finding what joy and beauty that we can in small things, and remembering that death cannot change love, may help a bit. To quote Dr. Halifax because she says it so much more eloquently than I, "The most defiant act in the face of death is love of another."

Eight:

Children—
The Forgotten Ones

The truth is that most of us do not do a very good job of talking about death even to adults. We tend to avoid emotional areas, try to make things OK, and use euphemisms as if saying the word "dead" is pornographic. The corpse is placed in a "slumber room" and covered with an inch of make-up so it looks natural. Our society sees mourning as an event to be resolved or overcome, as opposed to a journey that needs to be experienced.

It is no wonder children are often the forgotten ones when there has been a death. We do not intentionally overlook them but the child who has had a sibling, parent, or grandparent die, gets lost in the shuffle. Also, many adults, even bright, well-educated people hold to the misconception that children need to be protected from the pain of death. Though well intended, our attempts to protect children may actually result in doing more harm than good. It also robs the child of the opportunity to build important coping skills. We are all going to have to face the death of a loved one eventually and we are all going to have to face our own death. Contrary to popular belief, death is not optional.

We are inclined not to talk about that which upsets us. But not talking does not mean that we are not communicating. Children pick up on our non-verbal communications; anxiety and depression can be sensed. Look how sensitive animals are to our emotions—do we expect a child to be less so?

When I worked at the AIDS hospice we got a dog from the local animal shelter. His name was Innocent and he was anything but. He was the most remarkable and loving creature. His sensitivity never ceased to astound me. If someone was in pain he would sit quietly at the foot of their bed. Those who were healthier would find Innocent stealing their socks or jumping on the bed. When someone was dying he would come and get me if their breathing altered. Following a death we would clean the room and strip and disinfect the bed. Innocent would sit for several hours at the doorway as if he was guarding the transition from life to death.

Talking to children about death does not harm them. Deception and secretes, however, can. My experience has been that many people say they fear upsetting children. Often the real motivation behind the excuse of not talking to children about death is because it is painful for us, the adults.

I remember one experience in an emergency room where a mother was holding her dead child. The medical staff were attempting to get the mother away from the body. The unit was not crowded the mother was not posing a risk for anyone. It was simply that it was too painful to watch. It would be easier if the mother was grieving away in the lobby and the child's body sent to the morgue. But easier would not have been better for that mother. They should have been placed in a private location and the mother given the opportunity to hold the child and even bathe her.

When I was a doctoral student in Southern Illinois University I was a hospice volunteer. It amazed me how perceptive children were about death. A young child is unable to comprehend an abstract concept like death. It is not until they are much older that they can grasp that death is final, inevitable, and universal. This is a concept that is even difficult for some adults to understand! Please remember this: even though children may not fully comprehend what is happening, they try. I suggest we honor and address this effort.

I believe that a child needs to be told when they are dying. The parents may not be able to do this and that is understandable, but someone needs too. Being honest and direct with the child and eliminating secrets will result in a decrease in anxiety. Even young children can sense the pain and anxiety behind the façade of a smile. They sense dishonesty and discrepancy. The art work of children who are dying and who have not been given the opportunity to talk about it is often filled with symbols of pain (blood, needles, IV bags, tears) and anxiety (dark, swirling clouds, deep water, monsters, dark caves). When given the opportunity to talk about their death there are often marked changes in their art work. Monsters are transformed into butterflies and angels, pastel colors replace reds and blacks, and the themes reflect less fear and anxiety. One research study interviewed parents of children who died. Not one parent who talked with their child about death had regrets. Discussing death helps the parents feel that they did everything they could do emotionally to help.

We tend to underestimate the awareness that children who are dying have. On a unit for children with leukemia I had opportunities to sit in a dayroom and color with the young patients. Once I heard a child tell his playmate that he was dying but reminded him not to mention it to his parents or the doctor because "It would upset them." One thin, bald child told me that he saw them take his friend out that morning in a body bag. He said, "I think I am next." When I asked him how he felt about that he said he was OK with it but that his mother had been telling him he was going to get better and he hated to let her down.

When I was working in private practice in Richmond years ago, I had more than one adult in therapy because they had a parent or sibling who died in childhood. One individual was sent away to a relative's house for the summer. When he returned his brother had died of leukemia and been buried. He never had the opportunity to say goodbye, participate in the funeral, or mourn. This still haunted him fifty years later. Not allowing children to be involved in the death of a loved one can result in complicated grieving that may follow them for the rest of their lives. If we do not mourn it can result in anxiety, depression, or impact our ability to trust others.

We rarely give children time to talk about their fears, reactions, or feelings following the death of a loved one. It would actually be easier for me to get into the elementary schools here in Williamsburg to talk about sex than it would to talk about death. But children need to ask questions, even though many questions about death we are not able to answer. They need information appropriate for their age. If a sibling has died the parents may be too distraught to have these discussions with the child. This is when a grandparent, aunt, or friend of the family might need to temporarily step in. Again, do not assume that a minister or rabbi is automatically good at talking about death. If religion is going to be a part of the explanation about death, it needs to be with the parents' permission and congruent with their belief system.

We should talk to a child about death the same way we talk to them about sex, directly, honestly, and without sugarcoating the facts. Use the questions that children have to guide your answers without burdening them with facts that are irrelevant for understanding the situation. Also, keep in mind that there are many wonderful story books for children of different ages that address the topic of death and dying. I strongly recommend the use of these books.

It is best to use simple language and be prepared to be repetitious. Children may ask the same questions every day for weeks. Remember, saying "I don't know" is perfectly acceptable. Children will ask questions about the afterlife or why bad things happen to good people. Giving the child the message that you care and that you are genuine is far more important than having all the answers.

Even very young children grieve, they just do so differently than we adults. They may be too young to grasp death but the disorganization and change that it brings strongly affect the child. There is no one, correct way for an adult to grieve or any orderly progression to be followed. It is the same for children. Some will show their sadness, others may not. It is not unusual, for example, for a child to want to return to school following a death in the family. This does not mean that the child is not grieving but that structure can give a sense of control in a world that seems unpredictable.

For some children grief may seem short-lived. This is often due to their lack of understanding of future orientation. It can take months or years for a child to fully realize the impact of a person's death.

Though not always possible, it is ideal if the child has the opportunity to say goodbye. Children who are uncomfortable going to the hospital or hospice should not be forced. If they want to go, prepare them for what they will see. When children attend funerals it is best that an adult take the child to the funeral parlor prior to the funeral so they can walk around, ask questions, and view the body privately if the casket is open. Do not equate death with sleeping. This can lead to sleep disturbances in the child. Remember that when a parent has died it is very important to reassure the child that there will be someone to take care of them.

Temporary behavioral regression such as bedwetting, a fear of being alone, stuttering, baby talk, thumb sucking, or night terrors, are not uncommon and usually resolve with time. Never punish a child for these behaviors. I think it is a good idea for a child experiencing a death to see a psychologist, art therapist, or family therapist even if only for a few sessions. Just like going to the dentist every six months can be good preventative medicine, seeing a therapist after a death may prevent problems at a later date.

Get the child some paper and a box of crayons. Drawing is one of the best forms of expression for children. Well, it is good for adults too. It can provide an open and safe atmosphere for them to explore their feelings surrounding death and the loss that accompanies it. As I said previously, sometimes words just get in the way. This is often the case with complex issues such as death and dying. Art allows communication that is non-verbal. Children too, benefit from memorializing the deceased. Making a memory box or poster can be therapeutic.

It is not unusual for a child or adolescent to blame themselves when a family member dies. Most siblings fight and a child may believe that they caused the death of a brother or sister by "being bad." It is good to explore what feelings they have about the cause of a death and to be reassured if needed, that the death of a loved one is not punishment.

When a sibling is dying the parents' entire energy and focus, quiet naturally, is on the dying child. This is completely understandable. However, the brothers and sisters still need attention. Again, this is where a friend of the family or relative can be the biggest help. The needs of the surviving children are just as important as those of the child who is dying. Take the siblings to the park, to a movie, or bake cookies. Spend time with them, reassure them, and allow them to talk about their feelings and concerns.

Maybe the best thing we can do for children experiencing a death is to increase the amount of time we spend touching and holding them, reassuring them that though life is unpredictable that there is some stability, and remembering that grief takes as long as it takes. Once I think about it that might be the best advice for any age. Like adults, children are unique and some reach a state of adjustment quickly and others may take a long, long time. Reacting strongly to a death is normal. Not reacting strongly to a death is normal.

Nine:

Death of Other Family Members

Families today are vastly different and significantly more extended than when I was a child. Divorce, remarriage, half and step-siblings are commonplace. It is impossible to place the death of other relatives (grandparents, aunts and uncles, cousins, parents, nieces and nephews) on some hypothetical scale of grief intensity. Yes, for most of us the death of a grandparent who has lived a long and rewarding life is more often less painful than the death of our sister. But what about the individual who was raised by her grandmother and who has not had contact with her sister in twenty years? The situation is likely to be reversed in the case of their deaths. There are too many variables to make predictions. When I am sitting with someone who has lost a family member my first questions are often "will you tell me about them" and "what was your relationship with them." Remember, people usually have a need to talk about the deceased family member. Even when the relationship was strained or abusive, most people want to process it and put feelings into words. If they do not they will tell you or it will become apparent in their avoidance of the topic or their body language. They may be more willing to share with the passing of some time and following the funeral.

There is a movement, still more popular in Europe and the western part of this country, toward alternative funerals for family members. Alternative funerals in general, give the family greater control and move as much of the process as possible away from the funeral parlor and into the home. My guess is that this trend will increase with time. Look how the hospice movement has grown in the last twenty-five years. There will always be those who are more comfortable handing the body over to professionals. And this is fine. Others, however, do not want a grandparent or a sibling whisked away, covered in makeup, and displayed in a sanitized room with generic, piped-in music playing in the background. I feel that most families are relieved not to be directly involved and some even consider the funeral an inconvenience. I am pleased that there are rare incidents when a family wants to be an active part of the funeral.

I do not want to come across as being opposed to funeral parlors—that is not the case. Some of the most helpful and compassionate people I have met work within the industry. The details of a death (wills, certificates, transporting bodies, etc.) can be complex and overwhelming and professional help can be advantageous. Most states even have strict regulations about where ashes of the deceased can be spread.

I am mortified when people are pressured into spending thousands of dollars for a funeral or casket. I have witnessed funeral directors attempt to shame a grieving woman into spending more money than she could afford on a casket, suggesting that attendees of the funeral would judge her love for her dead father by its quality. Fortunately for her, and unfortunately for the undertaker, I was present and very vocal. If someone is alone going with them to the funeral parlor can be one of the most helpful things you can possibly do. A calm, assertive, objective voice is a gift.

When my family cremates me they can take the seven thousand dollars for a casket and donate it to hospice. It infuriates me that the funeral industry lobbies legislators to make laws that all but prevent home funerals. We are a world of individuals and we need a world of choices. And if we stop to think about it, before the advent of the funeral industry the deceased family member was displayed in the parlor, the pine coffin was built in the barn, the grave was dug by the neighbors, and people lifted the casket into the hole and used their hands to cover it with dirt. The death of a family member was not handed over to strangers. Sometimes the more involved we are the shorter the period of mourning. Seeing death, being a part of the mourning, may help decrease the fear associated with it.

While on the topic of the death of a member of the family, there is a fairly new and growing body of research, much of which is sited in *The Encyclopedia of Multicultural Psychology*, on how grief can affect not just the family but entire cultures, and how this grief can be passed from generation to generation.

Long before the concept of historical grief was being researched I experienced it when I was an art therapy intern at Essex County Medical Center in Cedar Gove, New Jersey. I befriended one of the music therapists at the facility. Sharon was Jewish and her family lived in New York City. On weekends Sharon and I would bus into Manhattan and take in the symphony, opera, a museum, or a musical. I also attended synagogue with her which was a first for me. She taught me so much about music and I was able to reciprocate by teaching her about art when we were at the Metropolitan Museum. I was invited to her family's home for a meal one evening. Somehow during the dinner conversation I mentioned that my mother was German and born in Mannheim. Sharon's grandfather pushed his chair back and stormed out of the room. You could have cut the tension with a knife. The family apologized and said that he had lost many family members to the Nazi concentration camps. My German relatives came to this country before Hitler came to power and they were most certainly not Nazi sympathizers. Sharon's parents shared with me how difficult it was for them growing up. If they complained about anything their father reminded them how many Jews died in the camps and that they had no right to feel any emotion other than gratitude. This incident, fortunately, did not in any way damage my friendship with Sharon. I understood where her grandfather was coming from and tried not to take it personally. I can only imagine the horrors that he experienced and the grief he carried inside. Of course, it would have been wonderful if he had been able to spend time with me and get to know me. I trust that he would have eventually welcomed me at his table.

Historical grief then can be defined as unresolved grief of historical losses that can be transferred to the next generation, usually experienced by members of an ethnic group whose history included genocide or severe trauma. For example, children of Holocaust survivors show reactions similar to those of their parents even though they did not live through Nazi Germany. African-Americans suffering the aftermath of slavery and discrimination, Japanese-Americans interred during World War II, and Native Americans, are other groups in which this syndrome has been observed. In light of earlier comments I made about the advantages of sharing grief, some Native Americans are addressing historic grief through communal grief rituals, storytelling, and therapy.

If there is someone in your life who has experienced the death of a member of their immediate or extended family do not just call once and say "let me know if there is anything I can do." Call, send a card, visit in person, and offer to mow the yard or prepare a meal. If they say they do not need anything or do not want to talk, call again in three months and asked them if that has changed. If they still say no, simply say "if you need to talk in the future please call me—I will be there for you" and then drop it. There is a fine line between offering help and badgering someone. When the mourning family member does want our support do not limit it to one visit or one tuna casserole. Often survivors need more support six months or a year down the road. For some of us it may take that long for the shock to dissipate.

At first some will need to talk about the death and the deceased. They may have to do this many times and go over the same story. We do not need to have answers, to move into advice giving or problem solving, hide our own tears, or make the pain less for those who are mourning. Be sure they have invitations to go to the movies or out to dinner. Check that they are not alone on holidays. Sending cards or calling on anniversary dates does not cause survivors more grief or dig up painful memories. Usually these remembrances have the opposite affect and are greatly appreciated.

I was at a dinner party in Norfolk a few months back. The host had recently buried both of his parents; I think they died about a year apart. The wine was poured and I was asked to give a toast. Everyone at the table was at least fifty and everyone had experienced the death of at least one family member. I raised my glass and thanked the hosts, gave thanks for the good food and fellowship, and acknowledged the memory of those whom we loved but were not long able to join us at the table. The moment was not without sadness—but neither is life.

Ten:

Death of a Friend

It is true to some extent that "death is death and grief is grief" and I might even agree that the similarities between deaths are greater than the differences. There are many aspects of grief that are universal, housed deep in our collective unconscious. But it is true too, that there are hundreds of factors that dictate our response to a death—I have already given many examples. If we lose a friend to natural causes the mourning will be very different than if they die as a result of a violent murder or a suicide. A woman who has many friends and holds a rewarding job is more likely to land on her feet after the death of a husband than the woman who was totally dependent on her spouse and defined herself only as "wife." Though grief is grief, there are naturally, some qualities of mourning that are unique to the death of a friend.

When a friend dies it may or may not be more painful than the death of a spouse, lover, or family member. It is clear by now that one of the paramount themes in my writing is that it is best not to make assumptions. Logically, it depends on the nature of the friendship. I have many friends I consider family. The death of a family member to whom we were not particularly close is not going to be as painful as the death of our best friend.

When I was seven years old Lissa moved into the house across the street from me. We have been friends ever since. We went to the same schools, had many of the same friends, supported each other through childhood neglect, cried together over broken hearts, rejoiced when her children, my godchildren, were born, and held hands at more than one funeral. There is no biological connection but with good friends that becomes immaterial. Clearly Lissa's death would be every bit as shattering to me as the death of my brother. Lissa has been my friend longer than some of my younger cousins have been alive and I have no family member with whom I have such an extended, shared history, or in whom I have confided more. I am sure that many of you who have had a friendship for half a century or more will understand what a gift this is.

There was a wonderful article in *Ode Magazine* recently. It was titled "Grief is Good." I totally concur that grief is not easy, but it is good and necessary if we are going to be healthy and happy. It is not advantageous to push the pain away or to just "move on." It is hard to jump into grief and to face it head on but this is exactly what is required when we face any death, including that of a friend.

I know I have said more than once that we need to sit with the pain of grief and experience it, without attempting to make it easier. I hope this does not come across as trite. It is much easier said than done. Our entire being will want to escape from the pain of losing a friend. My hope is that when faced with death that readers will remember that the task of healthy mourning requires being with the feelings of pain. Sometimes knowing this and having been given permission to mourn helps. Most of us will have a time in our life when the grief is so pervasive that it is impossible not to live it. Temporary shock, a few hours of sleep, or being distracted for just a few minutes by the beauty of snow fall, are a welcome but short lived release. Though turning to sleeping pills, alcohol, or drugs is unhealthy, I fully understand why many people do so. Those who need to escape the pain are not to be judged. We are to meet them where they are and help as we can. Some go through their entire life denying grief. That may be their lesson and we cannot always change this.

Mourning the death of a friend can be a shared experience and it is only natural to work through grief with others. Again, this is a primary advantage of rituals. I have witnessed the advantages of sharing grief hundreds of times in therapy sessions and grief support groups. Knowing that we are not alone with our pain and that others are in the same boat can be comforting and decrease feelings of isolation. Unfortunately, when a close friend dies we may be robbed of the very person we would turn to for such a process. The pain and burden of mourning is usually easier when shared. Though we need to honor those who choose to isolate when they mourn my experience has been that this is the exception rather than the rule. People who are grieving the loss of a friend often tell me how alone and isolated they feel. And those who initially isolate often do so to process the death internally and privately. This may be temporary. After a month or two they may be more likely to accept our invitation for lunch and to talk about the death.

I remember at my father's funeral the family of course sat in the front pew. My father's sister sat on the back row by the door. There might not seem to be a lot of logic to this behavior, but symbolically it put her at a safer (read: less painful) distance from the casket. And when overcome with emotion, she was able to just step into the vestibule and catch her breath. It is much easier for me to watch a horror movie on the television than at the move theater! The principal is the same. It took my aunt much longer than the rest of the family to talk about her brother's death.

As with many deaths, that of a friend can leave us to face how powerless we actually are when mourning. In a society that too often prides itself on the quick fix and getting closure as soon as possible, the tasks of mourning face extra challenges. What about the friend who died in a flood and the body was never found? What about the friend whose cancer has metastasized to her brain and has left her unable to recognize or converse with us? Or the friend who died on 9/11? There are situations were closure may not be possible.

As I have said before, preventing fires, when possible, is always preferable to putting them out. If a friend dies unexpectedly we do not have the advantage of preparation. When we know that a friend is dying we can do everything in our power to be sure there is no unfinished business and that everything that needs to be said is said. Spending time together has an intensity, purpose, and urgency to it like never before. If we take this time to laugh, to look at old photos, to cry, to wrap our friend up in a blanket and drive them to a place where we can watch the sun set, or to just sit quietly by their side with a book, the heartbreak of death may be lessened a bit and the memories will give us comfort while we mourn.

When my friend, Carl, was dying several of us made a schedule and would take twenty-four hour shifts to care for him so he could stay in his home. I remember fixing food that he was unable to eat, struggling to keep him pain free, and waking each time he got up in the middle of the night. It was hard work. But after his death each person assigned to one of these shifts said to me that they would not have passed up that time for anything. It was filling a short space with as much living as possible. We still grieved when Carl died but I guarantee you that not one of us has complicated grief. Again, I am not saying that we can always be emotionally prepared for a death that is coming. One can still experience shock even after watching someone waste away for months. But the more we are present for both the process of dying and the actual death, the less likely we are to experience guilt and regrets.

Once a friend has died be sure to reach out, if not immediately at least when you are ready, to those around you. If you are fortunate enough to have a mutual friend who knew the deceased, take advantage of this. When I was young and ap-plying to very competitive doctoral programs in psychology I had many rejections before being accepted. For each rejection I would start another application. It was my way of staying positive and dealing with the rejection. When a friend dies you never replace that individual. However, attempting to rechannel our loss by making a new friend is beneficial. At first, though, you may have to force yourself.

You do not have to have lost a child or a spouse to attend a grief group, or to have a few sessions with a psychotherapist or counselor. The wonderful thing about grief groups is that for two hours each week you do not have to pretend that you are OK. Everyone will understand. Nobody will judge.

I have lost many friends over the years. Some of these deaths were agonizing to watch and others were less difficult. After Joe's death I only felt relief that he was out of pain. Some devastated me and others simply made me a bit sad. And some deaths I raged after and one I even laughed over funny memories. I was going through an old dream journal a while back and came across a photograph of a friend who died thirty years ago. Even after all this time his image blanketed me in sadness and tears fell as if it had been yesterday. The pain was not nearly so intense as it was when he died, and after three decades it passed quickly. I hope, though, if I am going through that journal with I am a hundred years old his photo will still make me cry. I do not want to ever look at his picture with indifference. The first time I experienced the agony of a friend's death I though I might die. Now with age and experience I know that I will hurt but also know I will survive and that the joy of life will return.

One thing that has helped me, and this may not work for everyone, is that I give myself permission to feel sorry for myself for a few days following a death. I am basically a resilient and strong person. However, to allow myself for just a short period of time not to be so is therapeutic. Also when I participate in the Walk for Life I think of my friend, Sheila, who died of cancer. When I make a financial donation to Williamsburg AIDS Network I think of Mark who died of AIDS. This is one little way I can be sure their memory lives on. It does bring up a temporary sadness but this will allow me to access my grief and decrease the probability of swallowing it. Think of the analogy of a tea kettle on the burner. If the lid is held down and the spout plugged, the risk of the steam exploding is great. But if we remove the blockage from the spout and allow the steam to periodically escape the pressure will be released and an explosion is avoided. Grief works in much the same way.

Eleven:

Miscarriages and the Death of a Pet

Initially the topics of a miscarriage and the death of a household pet may seem incongruent. The common element is that they both involve a loss that our society rarely allows the person to mourn.

First of all, not all women want or need to grieve as the result of a miscarriage, still birth, or an abortion. For some it may be a relief. But for the woman who badly wants a child and has previously had a miscarriage, this type of loss can be absolutely devastating. As always, it is best not to make an assumption but to ask each individual what her needs are. But it is unfair to just assume that all women do not need to talk about this specific type of loss. Too rarely is the opportunity allowed.

I remember reading that in Japan there are actually shrines for children lost as a result of miscarriage. Women can go to these shrines and pray or light candles and incense. My fantasy is that it also affords an opportunity for the women to connect and to share their experience with each other. This could be very therapeutic.

Though I think this is a wonderful idea and that sharing loss tends to make one feel less alone, a shrine with burning incense may not be culturally appropriate for this country. There are other ways we can reach out to women who need support following a miscarriage. In our medical system nurses are usually more sensitive to the emotions of a patient than other medical staff. I am aware that there are exceptions to this observation. Treating the miscarriage as merely a medical procedure can be insensitive and dehumanizing. Women who want the opportunity to talk about the emotional aspects of the loss and their fears about future pregnancies need a place to share these feelings. There are times when a sensitive nurse will sit and talk with the patient who has experienced a miscarriage. I am saddened to hear my friends who are nurses bemoan the fact that they are so overworked these days that finding time during their shift to eat or even urinate is difficult, nevertheless making time to sit and talk. However, each clinic and hospital should have support groups for this population.

We as individuals, friends and family of women who have a miscarriage, can give them the opportunity to talk about it—allowing them to mourn. It is really very easy to do. We only need to acknowledge that a miscarriage is a death and honor whatever feelings are present. It is important that we do not judge or attempt to lessen the sadness by reminding the mother that maybe something was wrong with the fetus and it is a blessing, or that it would be worse if the child had lived a year or two and then died. These statements may all be true but that does not make them helpful. Our job is to sit with the pain and sadness and not try to wash it away. If you know someone who has had a miscarriage visit or take her out for coffee, asking if she wants to talk about it. If she does, listen. You do not have to have answers. If she does not want to talk, respect this and remind her that if that changes in the future that you will be there for her.

Some readers may initially be offended by the fact that I would even address the loss of a human fetus in the same chapter with animals. Most likely, these people are not pet owners! Let me explain why I feel there are similarities. I am an animal lover and would never abuse an animal. However, I am concerned that there are more shelters in this country for animals than there are for battered women. When I read about some movie star purchasing a diamond collar for her dog I cannot help but think how far the money would go in helping a sick or abandoned child. But the reality is that in this country many people treat animals as if they were children and many of our animals have a much higher quality of life than children in third world countries. But if we are going to treat animals like humans then we need to allow people to mourn their deaths without ridicule.

You do not need to treat an animal like a human to be devastated when it dies. The death of a pet can be just as devastating as that of a human. The reader who has had a pet they love die, fully understands this. Recently I had a friend who actually went to a therapist upon my recommendation for a few sessions following the death of her cat. She had purchased the cat as a kitten when she was going through a divorce. It was a very dark period in her life and the little kitten was the light that helped to pull her though. Her cat was not just a companion but a symbol of help and survival.

My neighbor, Lisa, had a cat named Shadow. He was the most useless creature on god's earth. He left fur balls and dead moles at my doorstep. Everyday when I came home he would run to me, roll over, and I would have to rub his belly. It was a ritual that went on for years. When he died I cried for two weeks. I would drive up to my house at the end of the day, get out of the car, look for Shadow and start to cry again. My neighbor and I could not even talk because we would start to cry. I remember my brother saying that I cried more over the death of that damn cat than I did when our father died. It was true and I think it was because I liked the cat a lot more than my father.

Grief is grief, regardless of its genesis. The death of a spouse, a dog, the loss of a limb or a breast to cancer, and the end of relationship, all of these are a form of loss. The grief from each of these experiences needs to be mourned and honored.

Twelve:

Alternative Lifestyles

I believe that grieving is universal. White, black, young, old, agnostic, Jew, gay, straight, we all grieve. Mourning is strongly influenced by culture and can be very idiosyncratic. There is, of course, no difference in grief among the infinite variations of sexual orientation. What is different, however, is how a heterosexist society allows, or does not allow, a person who is gay, lesbian, bisexual, or transgendered to mourn. It is because of this that I specifically address this issue.

Because of my work in the hospice for people living and dying with HIV/AIDS in the mid-1980's I saw homophobia at its most vicious. We actually had to keep the location of the hospice a secret because of death threats. Other AIDS facilities in the south had experienced arson or having red paint splashed on the entrance. We trained the home health care nurses to park blocks away from the hospice and to cover uniforms with jackets. The workers from the funeral parlors only came under the cover of dark and drove the hearse into the back yard so the neighbors would not see.

As a collective, Virginia is still a very conservative, southern state. I have seen more than one medical power of attorney ignored for same-sex couples. I remember one heartbreaking situation with a gay couple of thirty-five years. One died of AIDS and the family banned the partner from the funeral and cleared the house of its possessions. They even took the automobile that the couple has purchased together. The sad thing is that in this state at that time, they did nothing illegal. Many heterosexuals who are not homophobic and who would never intentionally discriminate are just uninformed and unaware of what few legal rights gays/lesbians have.

The hospice was called once to pick up a young man down in Norfolk who was dying from AIDS. He had been living in the back of a car parked in his parent's driveway. They were afraid that they would get AIDS if he was in the house. They fed him on paper plates and with plastic utensils that they disposed of after use. They were very judgmental about his being gay. He was dehydrated, covered in urine and feces, and emaciated. I thanked the family for calling us and told them that he needed more care than they could provide. They were relieved to see him go. We got him back to the hospice, bathed him, put him in a clean bed with freshly cut flowers on the side table, and fed him some soup. He spoke very little and died a few days later. I actually believe that he died because for the first time he felt safe and cared for. He knew his sexual orientation was, maybe for the first time in his life, immaterial. This is all subjective I know, but I do believe it.

I still remember the first time I heard the words "AIDS" and "gay" mentioned at a funeral. It seems like a little thing but it was the first funeral I attended that was not covered in hypocrisy. It was a predominantly Black, Catholic church in an unsafe section of Newport News. I found it to be one of those rare churches where the parishioners were actually doing Christ's work. I attended one funeral where the family told the priest not to mention the partner of the deceased because the grandmother did not know he was gay and it would upset her. At the reception I sat with this grandmother and she asked me if I knew that her grandson was gay and had AIDS! Not only did she know but she was comfortable with their relationship. She said to me, "Love is love."

In situations like these, gays and lesbians have to find alternative forms of support and ways to mourn. Too often churches and biological families bar partners and friends from participating in the death or funeral. During the 80's gay men were forced to mourn in non-traditional ways. Gay men and their lesbian friends were the first to design memorial services of their own. At times these needed to be conducted without the benefit of a body or ashes.

I actually went to a celebration held by a man who was dying. He wanted to be at his funeral and for his friends and family to see him alive, not when he was dead. My friend Jim knew he only had a few months to live. We had a picnic on his birthday and planted hundreds of daffodils. He made us promise that we would gather when they bloomed and remember him. It was bitter-sweet but a beautiful way to honor the life and death of someone. Some of the most creative and spiritual expression of grief have come from the gay community. This is remarkable considering the adversarial environment that they often face.

Things are slowly changing in our society, but homophobia still exists. If you know someone who is bisexual, gay, or lesbian and dying, be sure to support their partner if there is one. It is OK if someone does not understand or approve of homosexuality. It is not OK to be cruel or discriminate against anyone who is grieving because we are not comfortable with their skin color, religion, or sexual orientation.

Thirteen:

Death and Psychiatric Care

The majority of us would choose to die in our homes. However, a review of the demography of death shows that we are most likely to die in a hospital or nursing home. I work at Eastern State Hospital in Williamsburg. It is the nation's first, public psychiatric hospital. Our clients are inpatient adults with every conceivable diagnosis. Over the years I have had numerous clients who have died while hospitalized and many who have lost loved ones while undergoing treatment. Fortunately psychiatric hospitals around the nation are moving away from the archaic medical model where clients were rarely allowed to mourn with family or talk about death. Under a recovery model, clients are empowered and staff are better trained on issues such as do not resuscitate orders (DNRs) and living wills. Because someone is in a psychiatric facility or under psychiatric care does not mean they do not grieve or are unable to mourn.

An individual undergoing psychiatric treatment and who is psychotic or highly disorganized may need repeated opportunities to talk about the death of a loved one. It is the same with certain types of mental retardation, cognitive impairments, and dementia. A one-shot deal is not likely to work for someone whose grasp of reality is tenuous. We need to keep going back to them, assessing what they have absorbed and what they are feeling. I had a client once whose mother died while she was under my care. I asked a family member to come to the hospital so that we could give her the news together. For a few days she talked about her mother's death then she decided it had been an error. A week or so later she talked about her mother in the past tense. Assimilating the death of her mother was a progression that went forward and back for almost a year.

Behavioral changes such as a preoccupation with death, disrupted eating and sleeping patterns, or increased anger or withdrawal, are not uncommon and can exacerbate symptoms of mental illness. With time, support, and sometimes medication, they will usually disappear. Family and staff occasionally fear that the client may "go to pieces" following bad news. What is perceived as "going to pieces" is often a healthy and necessary aspect of mourning. What better place for a client to grieve than in a safe environment with psychologists and nursing staff trained in mental health issues? For some the structure, routine, and consistency afforded by hospitalization may actually yield a greater feeling of security and a sense of being in control during the process of bereavement.

As in the general population, psychiatric clients vary enormously in their response to bereavement. Some suffer acutely, some take it in their stride, and others become more sensitive and insightful than prior to bereavement. For some clients death will complicate affective and anxiety disorders. Almost half of all clients who are grieving will meet diagnostic criteria for a depressive disorder during the first year following the death. Mourning, as mentioned before, decreases the probability of complicated grief. It is beneficial for professionals to know that there are many factors that are associated with an increased risk of complicated grief. Low self-esteem, depression, a history of substance abuse, a limited support system, a recent, previous loss, are a few of these factors.

Though not appropriate or feasible in all situations, encouraging clients to attend funerals can often help with mourning and allow them to be a part of the family and community. When it is not possible, I have had family members tape funerals and then view the tape with the hospitalized family member. Another option is to hold a second, small service at the hospital so that the client can at least attend this safely.

Of course group and individual therapy is helpful. One advantage of group therapy is that a client's grief is shared and may decrease feelings of isolation. Some of the issues that repeatedly surface in a group dealing with grief include the impact of loss on mental health, thoughts of ending one's life a shift in one's support system, and guilt related to unfinished business. In working with psychiatric clients who are grieving it is important to keep in mind there is a big difference between saying "I have nothing to live for," and "I am going to kill myself."

In general, it is best not to underestimate the grief of those individuals with special needs such as mental retardation, head injury, dementia, or schizophrenia. With some flexibility and creativity we can support them as they grieve and mourn.

Fourteen:

Physician Assisted Suicide

If the topic of death itself does not push buttons mentioning physician assisted suicide will. When I am speaking publically I would rather facilitate a discussion on abortion or politics than suicide, the topic is so emotionally laden. I take a deep breath and work on being respectful of everyone's opinions. But it would be dishonest of me to say that I never find myself frustrated. It has been my experience that the people who are the most intolerant to the option of physician assisted suicide are those who have never suffered chronic, debilitating physical pain or a clinical depression, and have no concept of what it might be like to want to die.

Even Kübler-Ross, who was no stranger to suffering, was adamantly opposed to assisted suicide. She believed that to take your life, even if you were terminally ill, would do karmic damage. Following a stroke that limited her physical abilities, however, she admitted to contemplating suicide. And of course most traditional religions see suicide as sinful. In many states attempting suicide is illegal. Those of us in the helping professions have ethical guidelines about doing everything in our power to prevent a suicide regardless of the conditions under which it occurs. However, the American Counseling Association recently revised its code of ethics stating that counselors who provide services to terminally ill individuals who are considering hastening their own death do not need to break confidentiality. So in and of itself, a statement from a client who is dying and is talking about hastening their death does not constitute serious and foreseeable harm. This is a major shift in paradigm for professional organizations.

As I am writing this book there is only one state (Oregon) that allows physician assisted suicide. The Europeans, especially in Holland, are years ahead of us on this issue. It is interesting that the strongest advocates against physician assisted suicide claimed that if those who were terminally ill were placed on antidepressants they would not want to take their own lives. The research demonstrates that this is not so and is a reflection of how little we understand the feelings of people who are dying. Choosing to die has little or nothing to do with depression—it is about control, dignity, quality of life, and the fear of pain and being a burden on others. Those of us who have worked in the field of hospice care have known this all along.

Physician assisted suicide is not taking the life of a healthy, depressed person. It is helping an individual who is terminally ill and legally competent, to end their life when they feel it is no longer worthwhile. Rational suicide is when someone who is dying takes their own life without assistance. The Hemlock Society has information on line about right-to-die issues and has printed publications that are actually "how to" books on committing suicide. They tell you what medications to collect, how to get your affairs in order, how to take medication for motion sickness so you are less likely to vomit the lethal dose of pills, etc. For the readers who are uncomfortable I simply ask that you take pause. If you were in that situation what would you want?

When I worked in hospice we had copies of this book in the house. Most people read them but I am not aware that anyone ever chose to take their own life. But if we step back from our immediate reaction and try to put ourselves in the place of someone who is in pain, losing their physical and/or mental capacities, and for whom life no longer holds pleasure, we might be able to see the other side of the issue. I found the book was empowering for people who were dying. I know that if I was facing death I would at least want to have the option of taking my own life. My job is to help the person who is dying make the decision that is best for them, interjecting my opinions and feelings as little as possible.

As I close this section I want to make one additional statement. Pain and suffering are often related. But this is not always the case. People who are suffering because they no longer have any quality to life are not necessarily in physical pain. To want to die is not always an indication of depression.

Fifteen:

Humor and Death

$\mathbf{Y}$es. There are times when humor and death are perfectly compatible. Life is sad and life is funny. Conversely, death can be both sad and funny. Granted, humor can be used to cover painful emotions. I try not to judge people when they do this because it might simply be the best they can do at that time. But there are disadvantages to hiding or swallowing grief—they have a way of catching up with us down the road. Glossing over pain is not always healthy.

I also feel that to avoid or deny a natural, spontaneous humor is equally as unhealthy. It might get us some dirty looks at the funeral. Humor is more likely to be appropriate at the funeral of someone who has lived ninety years than at the funeral of a child. The circumstances (such as the cause of death, collective personality of the family, etc.) will, in part, dictate when humor is appropriate. Social norms seem to dictate that laughter coming from the room of an individual who is dying or to greet someone at a funeral by saying "I am so happy to see you again," are inappropriate. We will do well to challenge these notions.

I believe that attending a funeral that is void of any joy or humor is potentially as unhealthy as the opposite—a funeral service that is all humor or celebration. It is great that survivors are happy that the deceased is in a better place but it is not good when someone's sadness is discredited or when they are shamed because they miss the deceased or are sad.

I am reminded of the wonderful movie *Steel Magnolias*. If you have not seen it run out and rent it. There is a scene where Sally Field has just buried her daughter. A well-meaning friend informs her that she should not be sad because her daughter is in heaven now. Sally agrees that she should be happy but that she is not. In fact she becomes furious and her rage is expressed at both her daughter and god. To try and remove someone's grief because they "should" be happy is heartless. We do not have to pull our hair out and fall to the ground to express our grief, but the reality is there is sadness when someone dies, even if they have had a long and fulfilling life. We can experience grief and relief simultaneously.

We do not need to have a clown reading the eulogy to express humor but laughing over a funny memory is healthy and perfectly normal. How many times have you sat through a funeral thinking that the deceased would have been mortified if they had known how serious their funeral would be?

Humor and sadness are both valid emotions. When someone is sad we should not always automatically try to cheer them. Often during group psychotherapy sessions someone will share something moving and start to cry. I encourage the other members of the group not to immediately hug the individual or to hand them a tissue. It tends to shut down the crying and that is not always beneficial. We offer people a tissue when they are crying because we are compassionate and want to help. However, at a deeper level sometimes we do it because it is too painful to sit with the tears and emotions. Conversely when we feel happy, even if someone has died, we do not need to necessarily mask this emotion either. Like the Chinese symbol of the yin and yang, it is a matter of balance.

When my friend Carl was dying it would relieve his stiffness if I massaged Deep Heat into his joints. By this point he looked like a concentration camp victim. Once when I was massaging him he looked at me and said, "Be sure this massage is therapeutic and not erotic." We both burst out laughing. I am sure the people at the nursing station thought I had lost my mind laughing while my friend had one foot in the grave.

In our society we too often assume when a survivor is happy or laughing it automatically means that they are in denial. What I hear is "She is in shock. It is just hysterical laughter." Or "They are still in denial; the reality has not hit them yet." Certainly, there are times when remarks like these are on target, but usually not. Because someone is not showing what we think is an appropriate emotion does not mean that they are not deeply shattered and grieving. Laughter does not necessarily mean someone is in shock or denial. I would think that the premorbid personality would be our best cue. Someone who used humor prior to death of a loved one is likely to use it after the death. People who use humor while living most likely will use it when they are dying. Usually, we die the way we live. Humor is a personality trait, not a form of pathology. I feel that the ideal funeral is filled with tears and laughter.

When my father died I really felt like I was sitting at a funeral of a stranger. He was an abusive alcoholic and I did not have a lot of feelings about his death. I had years of Jungian therapy prior to his death to address the abuse and as a result I am not even sure that I was sad that I was not sad. After all, you are supposed to be sad when your father dies. My brother, sister-in-law, and I were sitting on the front row. My father had been a leader of a boy scout troop in his church. The minister made many references to scouting. At the end of the service he said, "And now Wade is resting in the giant pup tent in the sky." To my brother's horror my sister-in-law and I simultaneously burst out in laugher. I simply could not hold it in. Even if I had been close to my father I do not think I would have been able to contain myself. I am sure some people were horrified and others thought we were just overcome with grief. It does not matter. My sister-in-law and I still find it funny to this day. My brother, less so.

Do you remember the old episode from *The Mary Tyler Moore Show* where a clown is killed by a stampeding elephant? If I remember correctly the episode was irreverently called "Chuckles Bites the Dust." Everyone in the newsroom was making jokes about it and Mary was mortified. She found the jokes undignified and insensitive. Of course, at the funeral she started to giggle and the more she struggled to hold it in the more it got out of hand.

There is a moral there—humor can be a safety valve for emotion. This is very different than denial masked in humor.
Not surprisingly, there has actually been some empirical research on what gives hope to individuals who are dying. Along with interpersonal connectedness and a strong spiritual base, was humor.

Sixteen:

Near Death Experiences

If you want to read about near death experiences you most likely will have to look in the new age or occult sections of the book store. Though I am not by any means opposed to new age or occult books, and some of the most interesting and profound readings come from these sections, I cannot help think that books on near death experiences are only in this section. If a phenomenon is not scientific it is banished to the occult section. We might not be able to verify near death events but this does not mean that they do not exist. There is nothing wrong with a rational approach to life; occasionally I am even rational myself! But our society has become so rational, so developed, so industrialized that we eschew that which is intuitive or hard to explain in logical terms. As a result experiences that tend to be perfectly natural for primitive and indigenous societies, such as prophetic dreams and near death experiences, are ignored. In many ways the more primitive peoples of the world are light-years ahead of us. We have the advances of modern medicine and can fly to the moon. But we have lost touch with our spiritual side, our dreams, and death is no longer a part of life.

Like television, much of what is on-line is garbage. However, there are times when I marvel at the gift of computers and the ability for people around the world to carry on discussions in real time. I know I too often take this for granted. I remember reading Michener's *Hawaii*. One of the early missionaries received a letter in which she learned that her sister had died. It had taken six months for the letter to travel from England to Hawaii. She held the letter realizing that for the last six months she had thought of her sister as living and well. Today we can be instantly informed almost anywhere in the world. One advantage of this is that people who have had near death experiences can go on-line into chat rooms and connect with people around the globe who have had similar experiences. They realize that they are not alone in this experience and can be affirmed and supported. It is truly remarkable. Where there was once no support or opportunity to talk, there is now a dialogue that is international in scope. The similarities among these near death experiences are intriguing.

I read much of the research on near death experiences even before I did hospice work. I always found it interesting but did not give it a lot of attention. When I was with Elizabeth Kübler-Ross she shared numerous, first-hand experiences about people who had been clinically dead for a period of time. I also had the opportunity to meet and lecture with Dr. Raymond Moody years ago in Williamsburg, Virginia. He was a delight—very down to earth and easy to talk with. It was not, however, until I started working with clients (and one friend) who had near death experiences that my interest became more than purely intellectual.

A few years back I was lecturing to a group of third-year medical students at Eastern Virginia Medical Center in Norfolk. My presentation was about breaking bad news to family members. Somehow the topic of near death experiences came up. It was interesting how quickly the students came up with theoretical hypotheses to explain these experiences. The primary explanation was the one we most frequently hear, that the light at the end of the tunnel is the result of neurons firing as the brain engages in its last defense mechanism. I gently responded that this is one explanation and in some cases may be accurate. However, it does not explain all near death situations. I than shared numerous stories where people saw things or receive information when they were clinically dead that a mere hallucination could not have produced.

How do you explain the person who could repeat verbatim a conversation that occurred two floors above the emergency room where they were being resuscitated? I think the most dramatic story Kübler-Ross shared with me was about a woman killed in an auto accident. She remembered leaving her body and floating above the ensuing traffic jam. Most people were just angry that there was a delay. But she came to one vehicle and a woman was praying that nobody was hurt and if they were, that they would find their way to the light. She was so touched. She noted the license plate. She woke and was in her broken body in the emergency room. She was told that her heart had not been beating when they arrived at the crash and had been trying to resuscitate her. She had months of physical therapy and a long recovery. She managed to trace the owner of the vehicle through the plate and actually went to visit her and to thank her. The woman remembered the incident. This could not be explained via a hallucination.

Because of advances in medical resuscitation techniques, the number of NDE reports has risen sharply. Maybe our image of death as the grim reaper will change to a more positive symbol like light at the end of the tunnel as a result of NDE research.

It really is immaterial to me what anyone believes about near death experiences. However, what is important is that we listen nonjudgmentally if someone shares this experience with us. We do not need to explain it in rational terms. Too often, especially in hospitals, the near death experience is ignored. Physicians tend to roll their eyes or make some condescending and dismissive remark to the patient about being under stress. If one of my patients with psychosis comes to me during a therapy session and says they were abducted by aliens, it does not matter if I believe in aliens. I can be empathetic and give them the opportunity to talk about what they may have perceived as a frightening experience. For many people who are dying, stories about the light at the end of the tunnel can be very reassuring and help to decrease the anxiety that is sometimes associated with death.

I have only worked with a few individuals who have had near death experiences. Though there are always some aspects of the event that are unique I too, have found several similarities. Again, the observations are by no means original—there is an abundance of research on this topic. People who are "religious" prior to the event become very spiritual but much less religious. For example, the one woman I worked with who had a heart attack and was dead for several minutes had been a fairly conservative and traditional Christian prior to this event. After, she moved away from her church and said to me once, "Buddha, Christ, it really is all the same. It does not matter." Some atheists who have had near death experiences came back saying, "I was wrong, there is life after death."

Those who were initially afraid of death no longer feared it. One patient even said to me that dying was really much easier than she expected. Also, these individuals may have significant changes in priorities and interests. In more than one case I found that this was not always easy for the family members. I remember one woman who was very much the social butterfly and prided herself on her clothing and jewelry. After her near death experience she lost interest in shopping and socializing. She engaged in what her husband called the "bizarre" behavior of getting up early to watch the sun come up. She also started doing charity work for the first time in her life. Sometimes changes are subtle but often the person who survives a near death experience is not the same person they were before the experience. At times this is more difficult for the family members than the individual who has had the near death experience.

Though I have heard of people who are revived from death having special, psychic abilities such as the ability to heal, I have never met anyone who claimed such. I do feel that these individuals are more aware and intuitive. These people often undergo sweeping transformations as a result of the experience—less concern with the material world, heightened sense of the purpose in life, and increased compassion are paramount. Prior to the near death experience many say they took life for granted. After the incident they view life as a gift and an opportunity.

We need to offer support for people who have been dead and revived. But, beyond that, I would go as far to say those of us who have not had a near death experience can learn how to live more fully and authentically by talking with these individuals. Why wait to experience clinical death to make changes in our life? It is interesting that those who have died are simply saying what the Buddhists have been teaching for centuries—increased compassion, release of fear, and living in the moment.

Seventeen:

Why Try to Explain the Unexplainable?

This is a difficult chapter for me to write. I do not want it to be some melodramatic ghost story. However, I am unwilling to write a book about death and not mention the fact that there are experiences that are simply unexplainable. It is because the mystical and extraordinary have been banished to the realm of the unscholarly that I have to acknowledge them.

There is definitely change in the air. Look at all the books on the shelves now that combine science and spirituality. There is actual research going on around the world to measure consciousness. I think this is remarkable. But people still roll their eyes when you talk about communication with the dead or the light at the end of the tunnel. Yes, there are fakes and charlatans in the psychic world. But there are fakes and charlatans in the field of psychology, medicine, law, and every other profession.

I was talking with a friend over lunch a few weeks ago. He is a political liberal, a Christian, and gay. He was saying how fundamentalists have commandeered Christianity and how it needs to be taken back from them. This is how I feel about the affect scientific reasoning has had on our thinking. Each time I speak publically and each time I write on this topic, I attempt to take back a little of what has been commandeered by science. In no way am I opposed to science. It is the lack of balance that I protest.

When psychiatrist Dr. Brian Weiss wrote *Many Lives, Many Masters*, his book about reincarnation, he was ridiculed and ostracized by many of his peers. My friend, Dr. Jim Windsor, is a psychologist here in Williamsburg and was a president of a local university. When he retired he stated offering past-life regression hypnosis and hosting workshops on psychic issues. This was as a result of a remarkable, personal experience with reincarnation. This once respected professional was referred to as the "Ghost Buster" by some circles of clinical psychologists. Fortunately Jim was at a point in his life where he no longer cared what people said about him and maintained his path. The professional organization would have done better to invite him to talk with them instead of ridiculing him.

When Elizabeth Kübler-Ross took photographs of the hills surrounding her cabin to send to family in Switzerland, the developed photos came back with a face of a Native American hovering in several of the shots. She was totally nonplused by this and said that he was one of her spirit guides and he often appeared to her in dreams. She talked as if it were an every-day occurrence to have a disembodied face pop up on a negative. The reactions of others were interesting—from envy of having such an experience (I was in that category) to accusing her of using trick photography. At this point he media tended to dismiss her as the old lady who had gone a little nuts because she spent so much time talking about death. My opinion is that as people get close to the truth they tend to get rejected by society.

There are many other examples but I do not want to belabor the point. But I refuse to say that I do not believe people when they tell me that they have had some mystical experience related to death. If I say I believe in ghosts and have actually seen one I am not going to loose my job or my license. And, again, I feel the need to state that my purpose is not to convince anybody of anything, other than the fact there are advantages to honoring the stories and experience of others.

Fortunately, I had the visitation from my uncle at an early age. I never doubted the reality of it. It just happened, it was just a fact. Having had that experience kept me open to similar stories from others. Even if my parents had convinced me that it was not a visitation but merely a precognitive dream, you would have to admit it was a remarkably accurate dream. Over the years I have read countless books and research on death and dying. Along with the science, I read Jung, mysticism, philosophy, Buddhism, NDE's, and reincarnation. I do not believe everything I read but my studies and explorations have kept me open to all possibilities. Also, I do not think it is possible to do hospice work for any period of time and not have experiences that are unexplainable.

The literature and on-line blogs are replete with stories about premonitions of death. Even if we have not had such an experience first hand, each of us knows of someone who has. Usually what people say to me is "I knew he had died. I just had a feeling." Some of these are dramatic like a clock that stops at the time of death or a quick, fierce thunder storm. A woman shared a story with me once where she took photographs of friends at a picnic using one of the instamatic cameras. The photos were perfectly clear except for her friend Linda. Her image was faded and blurred in the two or three photos she was in. It was not given much thought. However, Linda was killed in an auto accent on the way home from that picnic. The lady who took the photos realized then that the strange occurrence was more than chance. If we grasp Jung's concept of synchronicity that I mentioned earlier in the book, where there are acausal relationships, stories like this do not surprise us. I have seen synchronistic events so often in my hospice work that they would fill their own chapter.

My friend Phyllis went with her boyfriend to set the stone on her father's grave. They got it in the ground and the dirt shoveled back in place. She said, "Well, this chapter in my life is closed". At that exact moment both the doors to her car slammed shut. Phyllis was well versed in synchronicity and knew that her statement did not close the doors and the closed car doors did not make her say the words, but that they were most definitely and symbolically related. Her boyfriend was a bit spooked!

I wish more people were comfortable talking about these experiences. As I mentioned earlier, it is was not until years after my grandmother's death that I learned that she also visited my aunt and that she, too, smelled her perfume in the house. It should be a rule that after a death everyone involved sits and shares any dreams or experiences that they have had.

A while back I was at a dinner party and we had finished eating and were drinking coffee and talking. One of the guests, Beth, said that her father had recently died peacefully in his home. The day before he died he said something about a Japanese man who kept coming into his room, sitting on his bed, and talking to him. He described him in some detail and the visits did not seem to upset him. The family dismissed it as a hallucination or confusion secondary to his physical deterioration. She said her father died a day or so later. At the wake an Asian woman approached her with condolences. The lady told her she lived a few doors down and that her father had died just two days before the death of Beth's father and that she understood what she must be feeling. When asked what he looked like she gave the exact description that her father had given of the Japanese visitor.

I believe that spirits sometimes come to guide and comfort us when we die. I have even had experiences where people describe a relative they never met or one who died prior to their birth. Sometimes it is a beloved spouse or friend who died earlier, sometimes it is a total stranger but regardless, they seem to give a sense of comfort.

A few years ago I had a client die at the hospital where I work. She was both intellectually challenged and emotionally disturbed. I went to the medical building a few hours prior to her death to visit her. I walked into her room and she said, "Look in the corners of the room. Do you see the angels?" I said that I did not see them but that I was sure they were there and to describe them to me. She said they were tall, male, and had shields and swords. I asked her if she was afraid of them. She responded, "No. they protect me." She said they were going to take her away very soon and we discussed her feelings about this.

I remember telling the nurses that I thought she would die that evening. They said her vital signs were fairly stable and that she was passing urine, etc. and that death was days away. The next morning there was a message on my answering machine that she had died early in the evening.

People can hallucinate, have delusions, and become confused while dying. Sometimes oxygen to the brain is decreased, or medications can cause these behaviors. But I want to caution the reader. Even with dementia people can have moments of lucidity. It is best not to ignore all they say or write it off as psychosis. Acknowledge what they say and be cautious with your assumptions. Listen carefully and remember that some comments may be interpreted symbolically. I have heard many people who were dying talking about going on a trip. This may be a metaphor for death.

If someone is comatose prior to death touch them and talk to them. Spend time in the room with them, even if you just sit quietly and read. Move conversations that could be upsetting outside into another room. People who have survived comas occasionally report dreams or hearing a voice. If the comatose person is dying, it is important to give them permissions to die. Reassure them it is OK to leave and that they do not have to hang on. I believe that touch is important for the person as they die and shortly after death. That was one reason why washing the body of my friend Carl was so important to me when he died. Remember that people who have had NED's often see what is going on in the room where their body is. I act as if the person who has just died is watching. I touch the body and send thoughts of going to the light.

The number of friends and people with whom I have worked in hospice who have had visitations from the dead are numerous. I love hearing and collecting these stories. But if this is so common why is it such a well guarded secret? I think it is the fear not being believed. In this society it is a realistic fear. The good news is that people are talking more about such experiences because of the anonymity of going on-line. People can share without fear of judgment. I am not sure what my feelings are about the after life. But I have had and heard of enough experiences to make me believe that there is something following death.

Soon after his wife's death, my friend, Rick, woke from sleep to see her standing in the bedroom door. She moved into the hall. He followed her into their daughter's room. She stood by the child's bed briefly and vanished. Rick is one of the most practical people you will ever meet. He never had an experience like this before nor has he had another. He has no doubt it was real and that it was his deceased wife saying goodbye. It did not frighten or make him sad—he found it comforting.

My friend, Cyndi, lost her beautiful, sixteen year old son in an auto accident. A month after his death she woke up to find him sitting on her bed. He smiled and told her that he was leaving now. She seemed so sad when she told me about this. I told her I thought it would make her happy. Cyndi said that prior to the visit she heard him in his room and that comforted her. After he came to her she no longer heard him in the room. At an intellectual level she understood it was good he had moved on and he most likely had remained close for her sake. But feeling him leave this plane was devastating for her.

Does grief play tricks on us? Do people ever confuse dreams with waking reality? Can a wish to see someone again be so strong as to make us believe something is real that is not? The answer to each of the questions is of course yes. But why must we explain away every incident? It is because ghosts have been banished to the world of nonsense. Cyndi said that not one person other than me, accepted her story—not her family, her friends, not her minister. Maybe they were afraid she was going over the deep end or that it would be encouraging this behavior if they acknowledged it. If they genuinely do not believe it happened I would not want them to lie and say that they do. But I think the compassionate thing to do sometimes is to listen to someone's story without giving our opinion on its validity.

If you have had a premonition, a visitation, or a near death experience, and you know it was real, do not let anyone convince you otherwise. Search until you find someone who will listen without judging or shaming you. If we hear over and over again it was "just your imagination" we tend to believe it and doubt ourselves. When we are grieving we are especially vulnerable and much more likely to doubt ourselves because the entire world has shifted under us.

If you do not believe in an afterlife or the possibility of visitations that is perfectly OK. But when someone trusts you enough to share something like this please do not tell them they have imagined it. This is not helpful and you might be wrong. You can at least admit "It must have been comforting to you," if nothing else.

I have two friends Christy and Lisa. They have never met and one is a psychologist in New York City and the other a physician in Richmond. Both lost their mother to cancer. During times of stress or crisis they both wake with a piece of their mother's jewelry in the bed with them. One even moved her jewelry box to a location where it would take moving furniture to get to it to rule out the possibility of sleep walking. They do not often share these phenomena because people rationalize it away. Nobody ever says, "Wow! What a great experience. I think your mother is still watching over you and clearly wants to send a message to you that things will be OK." I bet there will be numerous readers who have had the same experience.

My friend Becky had a brother die two years ago. I never met him but apparently he was quite the trickster. Every so often something will be missing in her house—a spoon from the table, mascara from her purse. She laughs and says out loud, "Put it back!" and later in the day it will be in the center of her bed.

My Uncle Tommy died in the fall a few years back. I was out late the previous night with friends in Norfolk and slept later than usual. I had the most vivid dream. He came into my bedroom and sat on my bed. We were talking about the weather or something unimportant. From the top of his head down he slowly started to turn snow white, similar to a marble statue. I said, "Uncle Tommy. You did not tell me you were dead!" he responded, "Yes. And I have to go now. But everything is perfectly fine. Your aunt will be sad but I swear to you this is no big deal." I woke up feeling alarmed yet in another way, reassured. It was a dream; I know that and I have no doubt that I was asleep. But it was so vivid and had the same "feel" of the precognitive dreams I have had. Soon after getting up my cousin called from Jersey. My uncle had a massive heart attack that morning—about the same time as the dream.

Eighteen:

The Importance
of Ritual

I have some very strong opinions about funerals. If you are dying please plan to have a funeral. If you are healthy please be sure you have a living will, medical power of attorney, and tell your family and friends that you want some form of ritual when you die. Also, please consider having an organ donation card completed. I did learn a few things while I worked in hospice; one was not to put off a living will. They make things much easier for family during a crisis or a death. Wills and a medical power of attorney are easy and even if you go through an attorney, not terribly expensive. Be sure your physician has a copy and that several of your friends and family have a copy. It is not something we like to think about or talk about but it is so important.

My father is deceased but as a single man in Virginia, he was my next of kin when he was living. My father would not have had the strength to remove my brother or me from life support regardless of the amount of time and the level of brain damage. I was not going to leave that to chance. There are things worse than death and being on life support with a brain injury would, for me, be one of those. I gave my brother medical power of attorney, and had his promise that he would hold a pillow over my head if ever I ended up brain dead.

When I say that a funeral is important I do not mean it has to be a traditional funeral in a church or synagogue. It does not even need to be called a funeral. Call it a celebration of life, a farewell ritual, or a bon voyage or keg party. What is done is of little importance. That something is done is of the utmost importance. Our society has moved away from funerals and it is my opinion that this trend is unhealthy for us individually and as a collective.

Many funeral homes have moved toward direct disposition. You can even give condolences via e-mail now. I have actually read of drive-through viewing windows in funeral homes. Granted, this is better than nothing, but it removes the opportunity for ritual and offering emotional support to the survivors. Once I sat with a family that was so busy with their careers, taking kids to piano lessons, and soccer games, that they had difficult finding time to burry their mother. It is hard for me not to judge this as a sad reflection on our society.

My grandfather died in the mountains of West Virginia when my father was a child. He had been an electrician in the coal mines. They could not afford a fancy casket and he was buried in a pine coffin. The body was on view in the living room.

My father remembers my grandmother bringing in pine branches to drape around the coffin to offset the smell of embalming fluid. The experience was fairly traumatic for him, understandably. I do not recommend that we revert to funerals of the past. But there was one advantage to having a decomposing corpse in your living room—it made the denial of death a lot more difficult.

One of the most wonderful rituals I have attended was a weekend trip in the mountains that started with a ten minute commemorative service and the sprinkling of ashes in the lake. It does not need to be a long or ornate ritual to be moving and meaningful. I remember a young man who died in the AIDS hospice. He had no family. We had him cremated, as he had requested, and those who worked in the hospice put his ashes in the garden behind the hospice. I guess some might see this as undignified but we viewed it as a symbol of rebirth. I read that you can now (if you are very rich) actually have your cremains shot into orbit around the earth. Also there are facilities that can take ashes from the cremains and with heat and pressure turn them into stones that can be worn as jewelry.

I frequently hear people say they do not want a funeral because of consideration to the survivors. Actually, to not allow the people who love us the opportunity to mourn or celebrate, is a disservice. I might go as far to say it can be selfish. There are tons of research on the psychological benefits of ritual. Ritual has a purpose and rarely is this purpose as important as when there has been a death. Funerals, wakes, services, parties, bring us together to give and receive support. They afford the opportunity to remember the deceased. Also, they help with grieving and adapting to the loss.

I was pleased to see the amount of commemorative events following 9-11. It appeared that an extraordinary effort was made to get remains to the family members. Even if a box contained only ashes from the site where the towers had stood, it was something concrete, tangible for the family to take home.

Years ago a Russian submarine sank drowning all the sailors aboard. The rescue mission to retrieve the bodies took days, was risky, and an untold expressed. But I feel this time and money was well spent because it was important to the parents, wives, and friends to have a body to bury. The ritual of the funeral for these grieving survivors should not be underestimated.

I remember working with a woman after the Vietnam conflict whose husband was missing in action. The grief of the women who received body bags was no less, but they were able to adapt to the death sooner than those who were left without remains.

Some of us believe that though the human body is sacred, once death occurs there is nothing left but an empty shell. You can donate my organs when I die and throw the rest to the dogs and it would not be an issue to me. But I am fully aware that

I am in a minority on this issue. I am very cautious to show the utmost respect for the body when working with families. And I do find the ritual of bathing and preparing the body before the undertakers come, as quite beautiful.

It may sound a bit macabre, but I love walking around old graveyards. On a hill overlooking the river in Richmond sits Hollywood Cemetery. It is a beautiful, rambling cemetery established long before the Civil War when it was a twenty minute carriage ride outside of the city. Several U.S. presidents are buried there. Also, it houses one of the most unusual Civil War memorials I have ever seen—a pyramid composed of cannonball sized stones. I wander among the mausoleums and enjoy reading the inscriptions and dates on the stones. There is one row of children's graves with little lambs on top of each gravestone. All died within days of each other. I am sure it was an epidemic of whooping cough or diphtheria that ran through the city.

But I never get the feeling that the dead are present here. That, of course, does not mean that they are not. Over the years I have observed the care of some of the graves and you can see they are frequently visited. It is so important for loved ones to come and sit and remember. Some people are turned off by graveyards, others find their greatest healing there. Ritual taps into our collective unconscious and should be encouraged.

I wish we would bring back the black armbands that people wore when they mourned. It gave people the chance to ask about the deceased and the survivors to talk about their loved one. I wish people still pulled their cars to the side of the road when a funeral procession passes by. And I wish we still took those terrible tuna casseroles to the family of the deceased. Those were rituals and they helped.

Nineteen:

Care for the Caregiver

Have you ever noticed when you are flying that the flight attendant instructs us to put our own oxygen masks on before assisting anyone else? If you pass out from oxygen deprivation you will be of little good to the people seated beside you. It is the same with caregiving. When we are nursing someone who is dying, we need to be cautious that our battery does not die. We cannot jump-start others if our battery is dead.

The rewards of helping someone transition from life to death are many. We know they have received quality care and they were not left alone. We know their preferences and needs. Also, we can feel as if we did something and had some control. Even symbolic control is important in situations when illness seems to have robbed life of control and predictability. I have seen countless situations were a caregiver felt good after the death of a loved one because they had helped and done all they could.

Unfortunately, over the years I have also experienced heart breaking situations where an over extended caregiver almost put themselves in the grave with the person for whom they were caring. It is a hard balance. I have talked to many people who wanted to care for a spouse with dementia. This is commendable and what most of us would want if we had dementia or a terminal disease. However, when the spouse starts leaving the house at night wandering the streets, starts a fire in the kitchen because they forgot to turn the oven off, or when they become abusive secondary to personality changes, it can become overwhelming. The decision to stop caregiving in the home is often filled with guilt.

Taking care of someone for a week with well controlled pain is very different than caring for someone for a year who needs total care such as feeding and toileting. I have seen family members who were exhausted and sleep deprived. In several cases they lost their jobs because of the demands of caregiving.

The advantages of dying at home are obvious. We can avoid life-prolonging machines and medical staff that too often ignore a living will or a medical power of attorney. It is easier to spend time with loved ones and the final days are more likely to be in a psychical setting that is private and comfortable. It is wonderful when we can die looking out on our garden or bird feeder.

There are people, the exception to the rule, who do not want to die at home. Some people want the most aggressive treatment at any cost. Those who fear burdening their family often choose to die in the hospital. I talked with an elderly woman who wanted to die in the hospital so that her two, adult sons would not have to bathe and toilet her. It was a matter of dignity and privacy for her. Also, I have heard of mothers with teenagers or children at home who feared that it would be the child who would find them dead in their bed. They wanted to spare the child that trauma and experience.

All caregivers should be given a bill of rights. They have the right to live their own life and to know that this is not necessarily mutually exclusive to offering good care to a loved one. They have the right to choose a plan of caring that accommodates their needs too and they should have the right to be free from guilt.

The type of burnout specific to caregiving is often referred to in the literature as "compassion fatigue." I think that is a very apt description. There are some simple ways to decrease the probability of compassion fatigue. One of the best things to do is to delegate to others when possible. What can friends, neighbors, other family, volunteers, and congregation members from the church or synagogue do to help? Having a few meals prepared and brought to the home or simply relieving caregivers so they can go out to a movie is a big help. The larger the support system, the less likely someone is to burnout.

Also important is scheduling personal retreats. It is not always possible to get away for a long weekend, but even a few hours will make a difference. I have a friend with a new baby.

The other evening I went over to her house. She had pumped breast milk and left it for the baby. She went out for dinner and some shopping. When she returned she was totally revived. Just a few hours make a difference when someone is dependent on us. There are times when I have had to encourage people to take a one hour "vacation" because there were few options. This may be a walk, a bubble bath, or a nap.

Having realistic goals is, in my opinion, the primary prevention for compassion fatigue. Often people will need our help in setting goals for care that are humanly possible and realistic. They tend to underestimate the stress of caregiving especially when the emotions of seeing someone we love die is added into the formula. The warning signs of burnout are many: decrease in weight, sleep deprivation, insomnia, headaches, GI disturbances, increase alcohol intake, forgetfulness, personality changes, irritability, anger, depression, or an increase in accidents.

The best advice to someone who is experiencing burnout is really commonsense. They need to exercise, eat nutritiously, and get sufficient sleep. Yes, this is most often easier said than done. This is where we can help—fixing a meal, relieving the primary caregivers so they can sleep or go for walk. Yoga and mediation are often helpful. Therapy can be wonderful but often a thirty minute cup of coffee with an empathetic friend is a life saver.

Even the best and most compassionate roles have a dark or shadow side to them—caring for someone who is dying is no exception. I have met exhausted, angry, bitter, caregivers who place themselves in the role of martyr. They become their suffering and define themselves by it, resisting any help. If it continues unchecked they are unable to perform well and the individual who is the patient suffers. The caregiver who refuses to show that they are afraid, irritable, or tired is in trouble. If you know someone in this position, pull them aside and gently remind them that you understand how important care giving is to them, but that they are human, cannot do the task alone, and that it is OK to give up some control. Assure them that there are others who are capable of helping and doing the job well.

Twenty:

Final Thoughts

If you are diagnosed with a terminal or life-threatening illness build a support system if you do not have one. If you are one of the fortunate people with a support system, strengthen and enlarge it. Quality and quantity of people in your group will be important. My experience is that retired people, without jobs and young children, are the greatest asset. If you need positive people around you, set limits with those who are negative.

If you are religious, turn to your synagogue or church or help. Pray and place your Torah, Bible, or religious readings by your bed. People with life-threatening illnesses often tell me that their faith is the source of their strength. If you are not religious set firm limits with insensitive people who push religion on you when you are your most vulnerable. Faith and religion are not necessarily related. Some of the most faithful and optimistic people I have ever worked with were atheists or agnostics. There are many levels of faith and hoping for a cure is just one of these. There is also faith that our pain will be controlled or faith that if we are going to die that we will not suffer.

Initially, there may be some shock and depression and this is normal. Most people work through this. When you catch your breath get a binder and organize your medical information—insurance, lab results, etc. You may need this as the illness progresses. Do you have a friend or family member who can be a medical advocate for you—someone to go to appointments with you and help you cope with insurance companies? There may be times when you do not feel well enough to do these things for yourself. When my friend, Carl, had to go to Charlottesville for the gamma knife procedures on his brain tumors we had a rotating list of drivers. This was a tremendous help for him.

If you are not assertive take someone with you to your appointments who is. The physicians will hate them but that is OK. Physicians do not have all the answers and some get upset when we go against their recommendations or ask for a second opinion. One of the best phrases you can have in your arsenal of responses is, "Let me think about this and discuss it with my family." When in the hospital it is ideal not to be alone. Medical staff are so over-extended these days that mistakes are common. To wait an hour for a bedpan is not pleasant.

I need to state yet again that all of us, healthy or not, should have a living will and a medical power of attorney. This does not mean you are giving up or that you are ready to die. It means you are being selfless and thinking of making life easier for your family. How many times have I seen someone die unexpectedly and watch their family go through hell? Where is the will? Where is the key to the safety deposit box in the bank? Where is the life insurance information? Do not put this off. Have your ducks in a row.

Again, planning for death does not mean you have given up. Do not wait until you need hospice to meet with them. You can plan for a funeral and still hope that the plans are not implemented! If your death will leave young children or grandchildren behind consider writing a brief autobiography and genealogy to leave with them. Letters and videos will be cherished in the future.

You have some control over living and dying. Try not to let the medical prognosis and lab results have total control over you. Of course this is much easier said than done. It can be devastating to see negative lab results.

Joining a support group or seeing a therapist will help. If you need an antidepressant that is OK. Some people with a terminal illness fight to the very end, others do not. You choose what is best for you. Remissions, cures, and even miracles do happen. Regardless of the odds it is human nature to hope for these.

If someone you love is dying, put your own oxygen mask on first. Your task is to help them without destroying your own health. You need supportive people around you as much as the person who is dying. Help the person accomplish some of the tasks previously mentioned. It is not easy to talk about wills and funerals, but it is so important. Death is difficult enough and we do not need to make it worse by facing decisions that could have been made months earlier.

One of the most difficult things for me to observe has been when a husband for example, is dying and had decided that he does not want to go through another round of chemotherapy and radiation. The wife, however, feels that there is a chance this may afford him a remission and that he needs to continue to fight. I can easily put myself in the shoes of the wife and understand her reasoning and frustration. At the same time my primary job in hospice is first, to be an advocate for the individual who is dying. More than once this had made me unpopular with family. I also have to put myself in the shoes of that individual—understanding his reasoning and frustration. Sometimes keeping someone alive is our need, not theirs.

If you experience the death of someone you love try not to let people or society fit you into some pre-established notion of mourning. It is individual. Do what you have to do for you and at your own pace. Be gentle with yourself and try to remove "shoulds" and "oughts" from your vocabulary. Depression and distress are common but not inevitable in grief. Grief can be transformative—we can become stronger and more empathetic. People who have suffered often have a unique wisdom to them.

Grief is a complex collection of spiritual, emotional, cognitive, and physical symptoms. It comes to us in many forms and the more we are prepared the better. Mourning can be agonizing but it is what we need to do. Never miss an opportunity to cry or grieve. If we do not mourn well we do not live well. I can trace anxiety, depression, and intimacy issues with my clients back to a failure to mourn. It might be a graphic analogy but grief is like pus in a wound. If the pus does not come out the wound does not heal. I have even recommended to people that they need to set time aside each evening to make themselves mourn. On the surface this sounds a bit sadistic but for some it is imperative. Forcing ourselves to think about the deceased no matter how painful can be beneficial—at least put on music or watch a movie that will make you cry.

If you are supporting someone who is dying, help them live until they do die. Do not "treat" or "direct", but go along as a companion on the journey.

If the process is wonderful and easy, be a companion. It if is hell, be a companion. Dying is usually a bit of both. Remember that you do not need to always fix things and make them right. We do not need to fill painful moments with words or actions. Being present to another's pain is not about taking away the pain. Zen priest Joan Halifax said "Being with dying often means bearing witness to and accepting the unbearable and the unacceptable."

Give everyone at least one opportunity to talk about their death. Just listen, you do not have to have the answers. If you start to cry that is OK. Touch a lot. People dying a difficult death need permission to leave and knowledge that they were loved. Everyone should be given permission to die. Let them know it is alright to go when they have had enough. If the family is opposed to a funeral or service gently point out the advantages of such and give some suggestions. If they are adamant against the idea, drop it and have your own private ritual.

Afford survivors with the opportunity to talk about the deceased. Expect them to experience all feelings; there is no feeling that grief cannot cause, including the lack of feeling. Do not ask a lot of intrusive questions about specifics—this can be upsetting especially when an auto accident or murder was involved. We do not need to know everything. It is all right to use the word death. Using euphemisms may be an indication of our lack of comfort with death. You do not even need to whisper when you use the word death! Saying for example, "I am so sorry to hear of your sister's death," is not insensitive. Death is death and there are advantages to calling it such. Sugar-coating it does not make it go away.

Do not avoid a funeral or a visit to the family because you are uncomfortable and do not know what to say. You can hug people in the reception line and not say a word; that you were there means a lot to the survivors. Most people will not be upset if you cry. Simply saying "I am sorry," "I will call you in a week and see if you want company," or "I am thinking of you each day," is good. Avoid saying "He is with the angels now," "God never gives us more than we can handle," "At least you had her with you as long as you did," "Everything will be OK," or "Be strong."

Dying is often hard and can be the ultimate cruelty. Conversely, it can be the ultimate gift of release. It is one of the most intriguing of phenomena and for many, one of the most frightening. The word grief comes from the Greek root of the word meaning to be robbed and bereavement from the word meaning to be torn apart. I think these are apt etymologies. Kübler-Ross said that the denial of death is responsible for empty lives. If you live as if you will never die you postpone things. Both the promise of death and the pain of mourning can result in growth and insight.

I am reminded of the book by Castaneda in which Don Juan, mystic and shaman, teaches that death is our eternal companion and the best advisor and motivator we have. Death is a primary reason why life has meaning and why life is precious. Death, Don Juan says, "Is always to our left at an arm's length. It has always been watching you. It always will until the day it taps you." Don Juan suggests that we look to our left to see and communicate with death. Through this process of acknowledging and discussing death it becomes more natural. And I suggest that through this process we can better face death rather than run in fear as it stalks us.